Dr. Richard Silurian MD

BabyShoe Publications ©
PO Box 75,
Sandwich, Kent,
CT13 9RT, England.

ISBN 1 874069 05 0

CONTENTS:

* * *

Introduction

The introduction to this book has one purpose only. To issue advice and

A SERIOUS WARNING.

There is absolutely no substitute for proper, informed and thorough medical care. No-one who is ill or has even the suspicion of being less than one hundred per cent fit should start on a training or unsupervised health programme. Any man who is impotent should most certainly talk to his doctor,.. or another doctor elsewhere if confidentiality is in question. He should seek expert help either from his family physician or via him from a more highly qualified specialist if needed.

This book does not attempt to be a substitute for adequate professional medical care. No such substitute is possible.

The aim of the book is to provide information and guidance. It should be read as well as and alongside gaining access to full professional supervision.

If you are impotent then see your doctor.

YOU HAVE BEEN WARNED!

* * *

Chapter One

THE NATURE OF THE BEAST

There is no known better way to treat and put an end to a man's impotence than to ensure he can have sex within minutes of choosing to. And that is what this programme can do. There are no ifs or buts. There are no half-promises, hidden clauses, problems or expenses. There is no more outlay needed than the time to read this short book and practice its techniques.

As you read you will discover that crippling and humiliating though impotence is, it can be overcome in almost every case. The Twenty Minute Miracle Method is an astonishing short cut to successful sex. Yet even it can be improved upon. There are ways to prepare for its remarkable impact that even further enhance its success. There are training routines that increase the odds. There are magical extras, unknown to all but a few doctors and wealthy people, that can re-tune your entire sexual system. There are ways to enlarge the male organ and tighten the female one too,.. and make both more sensitive and more thrilling to each partner. There are loads of sexual ideas and tricks that can improve your entire sex-life. There is information that can broaden your entire view of sex and everything to do with it.

And all this goes for women as well as men!

All of these things amplify the already astonishing success rate of the Miracle Method. Yet they are, for the most part, easy, do-it-yourself techniques. At a general estimate a massive one third of impotence sufferers will achieve erection within the first half-dozen episodes of intercourse by the method. Using the preliminary training routines and the magical extras the figure goes up to two thirds. That is already a success rate undreamed of twenty years ago. And it doesn't end there.

If all else fails there are still other methods that can be used to combat impotence. You will find them here explained in detail too. Added up it seems fair to estimate that upwards of an enormous ninety five per cent of impotent men can be helped, improved or totally cured by using the methods contained in this book.

And all should be able to have sex,.. and enjoy it.

* * *

Dr. Arthur Daniker is a world-renowned MD who is founder and director of a prominent sexual therapy facility. Read what he has to say:-

"Impotence is one ailment that really dampens a man's pride and enjoyment of life. It can be utterly shattering to realise that you just can't perform any more. Impotence is a health problem of huge proportions concerning millions, yes millions of men whose sex lives range from repeatedly disappointing to totally disastrous.

"But my research and experience has proven that any man can make himself immune to the heart-break of impotence. There really is a way,.. an astounding antidote to the crisis of impotence. It is rightly called the Twenty Minute Miracle because it works wonders in the first twenty minutes,.. faster than most aspirins!"

The doctor added to his remarks on the subject with a quotation from one of his own patients. It is typical of many similar comments:-

"It happened so fast,.. just like the doctor said it would. Suddenly I was able to do it,.. to perform, please my wife,.. it was just wonderful to have sex really again after all these years."

Finally Dr. Daniker said,

"I agree with the doctors who contributed to this book in their urgings that every man should discuss his sexual difficulties with his doctor. Nevertheless many will not. Whether they choose to or otherwise, the value of a concise, easy-to-use, at-home guide is indisputable. In my opinion the Twenty Minute Method is the best at-home impotence therapy I've ever seen. It reaches out especially to those millions of sufferers who are too embarrassed to seek help from a doctor."

Although I do not personally know Dr. Daniker, before compiling this book, I, the present writer, worked for almost thirty years in Sexual Medicine. During that time I encountered many different ideas and treatments. The best of them are gathered together here and in the other books in this series. And the Miracle Method is by far the easiest and fastest of them all.

* * *

Surprises in Store

This book is almost certain to shock you. It does not hesitate to make suggestions, propose ideas or to use language that accurately represents the facts. Some of the biological information and the logical deductions will be new and surprising to you. Some of the tricks and ideas will raise your eyebrows. Some of the proposals will literally astonish most readers. But the aim of the book is to jam a crowbar into closed minds, to enlighten uninformed ones, and to reveal to all a new, alternative and better method of thinking.

It is worth all that as a great deal is at stake. A sexually unsatisfactory relationship is an unfulfilled relationship. It is also a vulnerable relationship. Deep down men and women both need to give and receive attention. Attention given to others is a biological fact of life and is called 'grooming'. Its purpose in nature is to help individuals get along together in a group or a society instead of being constantly in counter-productive competition. In humans this basic, instinctive need for attention has been evolved to a much higher, but equally vital level. We alone have achieved affection and love. We all need these too.

There is no more profound example of the closeness of a human pair than that they choose to stay, live and love together for life. Realising the advantages of this, nature conferred a great blessing as a kind of bonding or cementing to strengthen the relationship. Unlike the other creatures in our part of the animal kingdom who have brief breeding seasons, men and women are continuous breeders. Unlike the other creatures who have sexual contact only occasionally, men and women are capable of and available for sex all the time. Therein lies the great potential bond. Sex and sex above all, is the attraction, the foundation and the bonding of the relationship.

Sadly, the stupidities of humans have damaged that ideal state of affairs. Instead of being a natural, frequent and beautiful attribute, sex has been soiled and polluted,.. made to seem dirty and wrong. As a result of this confusion many men and women who all have sexual urges built into them, have also collected fears and doubts and guilts. These have prevented millions of people from enjoying the everlasting and spontaneous pleasures of sex.

We are now at a stage where all over the world, night after sorrowful night, couples lie side by side longing for the warmth and affection, the love and grooming instincts that they need and that should be theirs. One will want to cuddle, another to stroke, another to have sex, another just to talk. But their intimacy has gone. She is not interested,.. frigid, they say. He can't get an erection,.. impotent they say. The truth is neither of these. She is not basically frigid,.. she has been corrupted into fear. He is not impotent,.. he is humiliated into failure.

Couples who don't have a happy sex life have no foundation to their relationship. And if a foundation is not sound nothing ever built on it will be sound.

* * *

The Female Role

There are other books (Scc Sources List in end pages) that tell women how to overcome their sexual problems and such an effort is most definitely worth it. Here however, we are concerned basically with the male problem,.. with impotence and its rapid treatment.

Nevertheless, the woman's role in such treatment is absolutely vital. For that reason there is a separate chapter especially for her. Ideally any man reading this book and intending to start on a cure for his impotence by the Twenty Minute Method (or indeed, any other method) should let,.. perhaps ask, is a better word, his wife or partner read this book too. And ideally she should read it willingly and with an open mind,.. and be prepared to co-operate.

After all, the relationship at stake is hers too. She will want it to be better, for her man to be restored, for their lives to be happier. Any good woman will want that. And she will want to learn the tricks and feminine wiles that can help those things happen. There is a source of pride and reward in it for her too. For be certain, when an impotent man rids himself of his impotence and becomes a real man again, much of the credit will be hers. That must never be forgotten.

There is no truer saying than that although a man wears his erection,.. it was his woman who caused it. It was her gift to him,.. and his back to her.

So, with those basic assertions made and those basic assumptions understood and accepted, it is now time to read on and discover what the whole problem is really all about. But read on with a difference. For it is now possible to have a great deal more confidence in yourself and in the future than it ever was before.

* * *

Chapter Two

ALL YOU NEED TO KNOW ABOUT IMPOTENCE

Most of the time the penis does nothing useful other than provide a length of conveniently flexible tubing through which urine can be poured out and thrown clear of the body. During these long non-active phases it nestles, extremely well protected, in the triangular niche in the body provided by the curves of the two thighs and the overhanging pubic bone. Behind it, even better protected, lie the two testicles, mobile but retained within the loose skin of the scrotum. Further protection is provided by a bushy mattress of pubic hair. This careful disposition of protection has nothing to do with the urinating ability of the penis. The extreme precautions taken are to ensure that it survives undamaged during the hazards of everyday life, and remains always ready for those possibly rare occasions when its other, far more important function is to be carried out.

This other function of the penis makes it an absolute essential for the carrying on of the human race. Eyes, ears, legs, arms and plenty of inner parts can be managed without. But for breeding purposes, a penis is utterly indispensable. For it is the penis that will transmit the precious, stored male 'seed', the sperms, from deep inside the male to deep inside the female, ready to fertilise her eggs and start her pregnancy.

To achieve this occasional, brief and temporary function the penis changes from a short, soft insignificant pipe to a stiff, elongated, firmly-rooted tube. This conversion into a rigid, projecting rod is called erection.

And that is where all the trouble begins.

Construction

The shaft of the penis, the visible or external portion, is only about a half of its true dimensions. The other half, the root of the penis, extends back into the body beneath the pubic bone. Deep inside there it is soundly bonded by fibrous and elastic tissues to the ligament and muscle sheets of the floor of the pelvis. At the deepest part of the buried penis root three tubes approach each other and join. The main, central tube, the urethra, comes from the bladder and carries the urine when it is being voided. The other two tubes come from the reproductive system of which more in a moment.

The urethra runs up through the shaft of the penis, along the inside of its lower surface, to open at the furthest point with a hole, the meatus or 'eye' of the penis. Throughout its length the urethra is embedded in a long surrounding cylinder of compressible tissue called the spongy tube or, to give it its anatomical latin name, the corpus spongiosum. From end to end the urethra is lined with an inner, moist 'skin', the mucosa. This is a very sensitive tissue and provides strong sensations when the penis is fondled or when fluids are passing along it. At the meatus the moist mucosa ends and merges imperceptibly with the outer, ordinary skin of the body which is dry and thicker.

The spongy tube would be far too soft and flexible to be used as a rigid communication channel from male to female. Extra strength is required and this is provided by two other remarkable organs. On each side of the penis, and between them comprising three quarters of its bulk, are two other cylinders. Each runs right from the very root up to the shining pink glans or head of the penis. Called a hollow body, or corpus cavernosum, each cylinder is comprised entirely of erectile tissue. It is this tissue that enables the truly remarkable feature of the entire organ,.. its ability to erect.

There are other parts of the human body that contain erectile tissue. The nipples of both sexes, the ear lobes, the lips, and the clitoris and vaginal lips of the female are all able to erect. But nowhere is the degree as great or as prominently visible as in the penis. When it is in good working order, the young man's penis can go from totally flaccid, a diameter of perhaps three quarters of an inch and an external length of two to three inches, to fully erected at great speed. Then, at its fullest stand it may be as much as two inches across and in exceptionally well-endowed men up to ten inches or even more in length,.. and there are cases on record where this astounding erection has taken place within twenty seconds!

Function

What happens is this. The main arteries of the penis, the cavernous arteries, are in the corpus cavernosum. In the non-erect state they are constricted and carry only the small amount of blood required for regular supply purposes. Blood normally filters through the living tissues, from the arteries that bring it in to the veins that carry it back out, through countless tiny blood tubes called capillaries. This happens in the penis too but erectile tissue has alternatives. Blood can also pass from arteries to veins by two other routes. It can pour out of the arteries into large empty spaces called trabeculae and then into the veins. Or, it can side-track that route and go directly from artery to vein through special 'by-pass routes' known as arterio-venous shunts. It is through these latter shunts that most of the blood is routed during the flaccid state.

Exactly as in a man made fluid system,.. be it a canal, or a domestic water system, the various directions of flow are controlled by valves. In the penis these valves are millions and millions of tiny, unnamed muscles. Some are around the walls of the cavernous arteries. If they contract the artery narrows and blood flow decreases; if they relax, the artery expands and more blood flows. Other muscles surround the exits of the small collecting veins. If they relax, blood enters the veins and flows out of the exits from the penis very quickly. If they contract, they cause an impeding effect on the blood and there is a consequent 'dam' formed with blood retained in the body of the penis thereby causing it to swell. There are even more muscles within the shunts that hold the shunts widely open when in use, but closed down when erection is not required.

The trabeculae, and there are uncounted numbers in each hollow body, are usually more or less empty while the penis is soft. Also the arteries are narrow, letting in the minimum volume of blood. The by-pass shunts and the collecting vein valves are wide open to let what blood there is drain away quickly. When sexual excitement starts, within an instant, thousands of 'switches' are thrown and the situation reverses. The arteries open, the shunts close, and the veins restrict outflow. Blood gushes into the trebeculae which puff up and swell rather as when air is blown into a balloon. Swiftly the penis bulges and starts to rise and stand out,.. just as the inflated balloon does as its interior pressure rises.

Of course, while the penis is erecting there is a great deal more going on. After all, one of the most potentially important moments of the man's life may be about to happen. As far as nature is concerned, he is about to try to pass on his seed and create a new generation. Nothing is more important and everything is geared to it. Virtually every part of the body becomes involved in some way or other in the acts of erection and intercourse. Look at the list below,.. and it is far from complete.

Hair stands out on scalp and skin

Ears flatten against the side of the head

Pupils of the eyes dilate

The nostrils flare

Lips and mouth become drier

Lips swell a little

Adrenalin pours out of the glands into the bloodstream

Sugar is released into the blood

Blood vessels of the skin and intestines close down a little to divert supplies

The heart rate increases

Blood pressure goes up

Palms perspire

Face reddens

Pubic hair erects

Respiration becomes shallower but faster

External distracting stimuli are damped,.. cold, discomfort, and outside sounds etc. are ignored.

The bladder relaxes and the anal sphincter tightens

Semen pumps from store sacks and more oozes from the tube walls and is milked into the penis root.

And all the time this is going on there is an intense and mounting emotional or erotic response. Feelings like affection, love, lust, aggression and possessiveness mingle and compete in a tangled web of mental responses all with immense urgency and amplification.

It is possible to draw a graphic representation of the events that take place in male and female during the arousal phase of human sexual contact. This will aid those of less experience in spotting what is actually happening to the partner. Of course, not everyone reacts in exactly the same way,.. some seem to miss certain features and emphasise others. It is not possible to expect everyone to be the same. There are wide personal variations. But, broadly speaking, this is the usual sequence of events.

Other activities

As the early stages of the growing encounter are passed and more serious intentions start to become established there is a marked physiological response within the body. Some occur in both sexes, others vary. The heart rate increases from around seventy to eighty beats per minute to well over one hundred. Up to one hundred and thirty is not uncommon and even this is exceeded in the third stage. Blood pressure too rises from the normal 120 to 130 to approach 200 or more. Respiration rate increases though individual breaths take in less air than usual. There is often associated gasping, groaning and grunting. Blood is shunted away from the abdominal organs and into the skin increasing its sensitivity and creating a warm sensation to the touch. In particular, certain areas of the body become engorged with extra blood and appear more pinkish and swollen,.. ear lobes, lips, the flared nostrils, nipples and the genitals.

In the female not only the nipples but the breasts also enlarge and tend to stand out further and firmer. The areola, the circular area around the nipple, intensifies in colour and appears swollen above the surrounding skin. There is also a visible sexual flush in many women. In this the skin starts to glow a brighter pink starting over the upper abdomen and spreading up over the breasts to involve the chest and maybe the neck and face too.

During what is called the 'arousal phase' of the female sexual encounter, along with her rising sense of excitement, blood flow in the pelvis increases and the network of blood vessels around the vagina engorge. The outer vaginal lips swell up to double or treble size and this distension inclines them to draw apart. The inner lips similarly distending, pout out from their usually more concealed position. The tissues of the inner lips become a far brighter red and the cavity of the vagina itself relaxes and increases in length, and undergoes a ballooning. The woman is now in what is known as her 'plateau phase' which may be maintained for a considerable period. A rim of thickened tissue called the orgasmic platform can very often be felt forming around the lower third of the vagina.

Assisted by the surrounding muscles, this contributes to vagina 'grip' on penetrating objects. At the same time the position of the uterus in the pelvis alters as it rises up and comes more into line with the vagina. Throughout there is a tendency for the vaginal walls to ooze a thin lubricating fluid. The clitoris also enlarges and becomes exceedingly sensitive. At first the enlargement makes it appear more protuberant but as the inner labia also engorge it may once again disappear under its swollen foreskin.

In the male the penis erects usually increasing length by some eighty per cent from the average soft seven to ten centimetres to nearer seventeen (from something over three inches to over six). The volume of blood it contains may be six or seven times that of its flaccid state. The spermatic cords in the scrotum tighten against the body and draw up the testicles as the scrotum muscle itself contracts further lifting them and reducing their freedom to move. The testicles also enlarge during excitement and may as much as double in size.

Eventually, in the third or copulation stage, there is actual penetration of the penis into the vagina. As this happens the female vaginal muscles automatically relax to permit entry and a series of contractions starts in them at rhythmic, three or four second intervals. At orgasm there are up to a dozen or so stronger contractions at far shorter,.. about one second, intervals. This is almost exactly the same frequency as orgasmic contractions in the muscles of the penis root which powerfully ejaculate semen up the tube and into the vagina. The uterus may continue with 'after contractions' which are believed to help suck up semen into the body of the uterus itself.

Most women are able, especially with a little practice, to repeat their orgasm phase, often several times. This is seldom possible for men who at this post-orgasmic point usually undergo a refractory period of anything up to fifteen minutes or more during which further excitement is impossible and attempts at it even painful. Finally there is a 'resolution phase' of post-coital contentment though this may be preceded by a brief period of intense flushing and perspiring.

The control system

It is likely that all women and all men have the potential biological ability to respond to arousal in the ways described above. Regrettably some do not realise their potential. Desire and even interest may not be stimulated or that which once existed in the past may be lost. There are many reasons which we shall discuss in later chapters,.. anxiety, post-sexual trauma, guilts, doubts and of course, physical ill-health. Also, the effects of age unquestionably make themselves felt as we shall soon see. But these many causes must never be seen out of proportion to the way they really are. By meeting any limitations with grudging and delayed acceptance rather than at once and automatically, both male and female can effectively and extensively prolong sexual enjoyment and ability.

This entire process of arousal, erection, getting ready for sex and achieving its activities and eventual orgasm,.. and by now its overwhelming complexity starts to become apparent, is under the control of parts of the nervous system. The different portions work separately, but as part of an integrated whole rather like the smooth running of the many parts of a complex, efficient engine.

The upper centres of the brain experience the emotions of love and affection. The lower, more primitive areas are involved with the aggression and the urge to procreate. The nerves carry their electrochemical messages from the sensitive skin of the penis head, from the eyes, the stroking hands, and all the other body parts that are in sexual contact. The spinal cord and its 'telephone exchange' reflex centres are buzzing with activity. The separate autonomic nervous system is busy with its hormones, its blood flows, its blood pressure. The entire body 'orchestra' is being co-ordinated simultaneously in thousands of different combinations of alternatives.

This simple, brief act of erection then is anything but simple. The confusing picture just described is not one half of it. The subtle balances, rapid changes, shifts of emphasis of the integrated physical, nervous and emotional factors are complex beyond all description. And the phenomenal chemical and enzyme reactions induced and involved,.. and there are thousands, we have not even mentioned yet.

The wonder is perhaps, not that so many men are impotent,.. but that any men, ever, manage to get an erection that is dependent upon such a complicated mechanism. The possible sources of error are so many, so varied and so vulnerable, that it is really no surprise that things can go wrong as often and as easily as they do. That is the bad news. The good news is that things that go wrong easily can usually be fixed easily. And that is the case with most instances of impotence.

Vast numbers

One cautious estimate has suggested that in the United Kingdom there are about two million men suffering from a degree of impotence that can be classed as more than brief and occasional. That is a way of saying that two million men are troubled with long term or recurrent degrees of impotence. That makes it just about the commonest serious medical problem in the country. The estimate is almost certainly far too low. So is the estimate of ten million sufferers in the United States and twenty million more in mainland Europe. Either way you look at it it is an enormous figure. Just because impotence doesn't stop you going to work does not mean it is not a serious condition. It is. And its spin-off consequences can most surely become the cause of time lost from work.

In terms of sheer human misery impotence must rank close to the very head of the list. A man may build a house, run a successful company or write a best seller. But if he can't have sex whenever he wants it, he will still feel inadequate, unfulfilled, unrewarded,.. and very, very unhappy. For a healthy, successful man to enter the bedroom of his existing or proposed partner only to find that nothing he or she can do will make his penis erect, is about the most humiliating of all human experiences. And it doesn't matter how much he wants it. His sex drive and urges can be at full speed yet make no difference.

A woman does not have this problem. If she has no great desire for sex she can nevertheless be co-operative, and ensure her man gets what he needs. She can, as many women do, fake an orgasm in order to help her man feel good. An impotent man can do nothing. He can't get an erection. Or he loses it far too soon. And either way he almost certainly will not orgasm. He can't fake it,.. if no semen appears the fact can't be hidden. If erection fails he can't hide it. In front of the very person before whom he wishes to be an impressive figure, his weakness is exposed and held up to ridicule. He can't get it up. He can't cut the mustard. He is impotent.

It doesn't stop there. The actual word, impotence, carries other implications. As soon as he applies it to himself, these other associations start to operate. The impotent man is of low self esteem, low body-image, low confidence. He thinks failure, he thinks small. The impotent man is a pathetic, unsuccessful weakling. The inner belittling he suffers from this unconcealable humiliation affects him in many possible ways. He may retreat from sex altogether,.. say he doesn't need it. He may cruelly blame his wife for his disinterest and failure. He may counteract the failure with bursts of self-punishment or unduly aggressive behaviour towards others, picking fights, quarrelling, driving his staff at work. He may become ill-tempered, unsettled,.. shouting at the children, physically ill-treating his wife, kicking the cat. His health may suffer from the reflection of his anxieties. His blood pressure goes up allergies appear, ulcers develop. He becomes an introspective, agitated, frustrated man along with everything that entails.

Of course not every man reacts in such an extreme way as the picture just painted. But every impotent man has some of those consequences, often plenty of them. Fears and anxieties are both the cause and the result.

In spite of this most men with impotence never go to the doctor for help. They suffer and go on suffering. Approximately five per cent only of sufferers seek medical advice,.. less than two million out of the perhaps forty million in Western society. Furthermore, an equally unexpected fact is that of those attending for consultation, no less than a whacking great forty per cent had impotence of 'iatrogenic' origin, that is impotence actually caused by various doctors and their recommended drugs and other treatments.

Impotence in history

The causes of impotence are many and the men affected with such misery are represented throughout the entire spectrum of society's history and geography. There are records in ancient Egyptian papyri of aphrodisiacs and of treatment for impotence. We know too that at the height of Greek civilisation they prescribed treatments for impotence. So did the citizens of Pompeii and doubtless the rest of the far flung Roman Empire. In 17th and 18th century London there were quacks and charlatans galore,.. much like today, trying everything from magnetism therapy and crushed pearls to hypnosis and the distilled, sweet breath of known virgins. Napoleon was a sufferer. So was Caesare Borgia. So were Leo Tolstoy and Mark Twain. George III of England wore a penis energising ring (See Chapter Six) and later Queen Victoria's consort wore his Prince Albert Ring through the head of his penis. Winston Churchill underwent several episodes of impotence, and so did Pope Pius VI,.. though how anyone could tell is not apparently recorded! This present writer could draw up a list of VIPs he has treated. On it there would be many recognisable names that would astonish readers for they are well-known, powerful and active men prominent in public life. They included governors, ministers, members of the House of Lords, princes of industry, popular entertainers and senior officers of all three services. Following their treatment, it is fondly imagined that the majority at least of these are now enjoying a better life,.. and their wives a happier one.

The causes

Opinions vary widely as to what proportion of impotence cases are caused by physical and disease factors and what proportion by emotional ones. Ten years ago some ninety per cent were accepted as having 'psychological' causes. Today the estimate is that sixty per cent have either primarily physical causes or causes in which there is a physical aspect too. The distinction makes a difference as lines of treatment vary. However it must be born in mind that emotional causes can produce physical results; even more so physical impotence also brings with it emotional responses. In the vast majority of cases experience has shown that mental and physical causes are seldom as widely separated as some experts believe,.. and generally there are aspects of both in each instance.

Either way the agonies and mental stresses, the fears and the anxieties, have to be contended with by every individual sufferer. As one wit put it, anxiety is the first time you can't do it the second time. Fear is the second time you can't do it the first time!

The diseases which either cause or are associated with impotence make a tremendous and alarming list. Basically four causes are recognised,.. those to do with circulation, those to do with neurological (nerve) diseases, those of hormonal origin, and the huge number of psychological causes. Below is a list which is by no means complete:-

Neurological:

Alzheimer's Disease
Brain Surgery
Peripheral Neuropathy
Pituitary Tumours
Cerebrovascular Accidents (strokes etc)
Multiple Sclerosis
Parkinson's Disease
Spina Bifida
Spinal Cord Injury
Temporal Lobe Epilepsy

Circulatory:

Ageing
Angina
Atherosclerosis
Congestive Heart Failure
Obstruction
Priapism

Hormonal and Metabolic:

Acromegaly
Addisons Disease
Cushing's Syndrome
Diabetes
Pituitary Tumours
Testicular Tumours
Hormone imbalances
Systemic Diseases
Cirrhosis
Kidney Failure

Surgical and Traumatic:

Abdominoperineal Surgery
Pelvic Surgery

Pelvic Fractures
Pelvic Radiation Therapy
Penis Trauma
Prostatectomy
Renal Transplantation
Sympathectomy

Urological:

Cystitis
Hypospadias
Peyronie's Disease
Phimosis
Prostatitis
Urethritis

A serious warning

If you (or your partner) suffer from any of these conditions and you have an impotence problem however slight, you should most certainly inform your doctor and see what can be done to help matters. This factor stresses the advice given at the start of this book and throughout it, that nothing, not even a book as detailed as this, and not even the Twenty Minute Method, should be regarded as a substitute for proper, skilled medical advice. This should be regarded as a valuable warning. For most of the conditions listed there is available a sound medical treatment, often even a cure. It is in your interest to find out from your doctor as no further help may then be needed. Or, without that help, no other technique may work meaning that all your efforts would be a fruitless waste of time, money and effort. The message is simple,.. see your doctor too.

Having again stressed that advice, there is an associated warning to be added. Perhaps as many as forty per cent of those men who do seek medical advice for their impotence eventually find out that the cause of that impotence was, in fact, the doctor and his treatment for some other problem. When questioned, a disturbing proportion of doctors just didn't know of the connection between impotence and many drugs and diseases, or if they had once known they had forgotten. The general public opinion is that the majority of doctors understand more about sex and have more sexual experience than other folk. It is a sad fact, but a fact nonetheless, that this is simply not the case. Indeed, as a group, non-specialist doctors tend to have a lower than average knowledge and experience in sexual matters. Furthermore, professional studies have clearly shown that doctors are, again as a group, amongst those people who have great difficulty coming to terms with their own sexuality. The problems of sex and sexuality amongst doctors comprise a largely unexplored area. This merits closer investigation in view of the problems and consequences that arise both personally and professionally.

There are innumerable cases, for example, where doctors have assumed that correcting a man's blood pressure is more important to that man than the fact that the very drugs used to control the pressure will make him impotent. Because high blood pressure is potentially life-threatening they give it every priority. Some are too embarrassed to discuss the matter. So, they don't ask, and very often don't even tell. They take it for granted that the patient will agree his blood pressure is more important than his sex-life. They are frequently wrong. Many men prefer their potency left intact and their illness treated another way or not at all. Many men, not knowing why they have become impotent, become so worried that their entire lives, business and families suffer. In short they may become more ill and have their quality of life more damaged by their iatrogenic impotence, than ever could have resulted from their blood pressure. Below is an incomplete list of medications that can cause or are associated with impotence. If you are on any of them, it may be the cause of your trouble. Talk to your doctor about it soon. (NB.Trade-names marked with 'R').

Anti-anxiety agents:

Librium R
Tranxene R
Valium R
Miltown R
Equanil R

Antihistamines:

Anti-Parkinsonism Drugs:
Kemadrin R

Antispasmodics:

Pro-Banthine R
Atropine

Muscle Relaxants:

Norflex R

Anti-Depressants:

Marplan R
Nardil R
Parnate R
Norprimine R
Sinequan R
Tofranil R
Aventyl R

Antihypertensives:

Lopressor R

Beta Blockers:

Inderal R
Minipres R
Aldomet R
Serpasil R
Hygroton R
Guanethidine (Ismelin R)
Apresoline R
Sparine R
Melleril R

Drugs with abuse potential:

Alcohol
Amphetamines
Barbiturates
Cocaine
Marijuana
Narcotics
Nicotine

Opiates

Miscellaneous:

Tagamet R
Atromid-S R
Digoxin
Indocid R
Lithium carbonate
Flagyl R

Starting the diagnosis

The diagnosis of the different kinds of causes of impotence is a skilled matter. Few general physicians would attempt it. However a good guide is to be found in the following lists. It is pointed out that these are not complete diagnostic lists. There is no such thing. However, any man with impotence and exhibiting a substantial number of the features in the list, should consider that classification the one in which he probably belongs. It must be remembered that it is possible to belong in more than one group. For instance a man with diabetic impotence may also have his condition associated with, complicated by or even preceded by an element of emotional cause.

Factors and symptoms involved in impotence:

Hormonal:

Patient is usually over sixty.
The condition is progressive.
There is loss of sexual interest.
Impotence happens in all scenarios and with all partners.
There are few or no sexual fantasies.
There are no erotic or 'wet' dreams.
Sex is rarely initiated by patient.
There may be loss of beard growth.
Testicles small or smaller than previously.

Neurological:

Impotence with partner and during masturbation.
Few or no morning erections.

Few or no nocturnal erections.
Tendency to postural hypotension.
Urinary bladder weakness.
Occasional diarrhoea.
History of injury.
History of surgery in pelvic region.
Known diabetic.

Circulatory:

Gradual onset.
History of impotence after alcohol.
Impotent with partner and during masturbation.
No morning erections.
No nocturnal erections.
Cold feet and hands.
Cold penis.
Partly erect penis 'bends' in the middle.
Pain in legs on walking.
Known circulatory disease.
Diminished erectile response to erotic/pornographic material.

Psychological;

Sudden onset.
Intermittent episodes.
Present with certain partners only.
Present mostly or only when attempting intercourse.
Good erections during masturbation.
Morning erections present.
Nocturnal erections present.
Experiences of anxiety and tension.
Relationship problems present.
Poor communication skills.
Restrictive upbringing.
Prominent sexual myths and taboos.
No known, or signs of, physical illness.

Nature v. Nurture

Despite all these listed physical and disease factors, an immense group of causes still lie in the emotional-psychological realm. Why should this be so?

As might be expected the reasoning is complex and based upon widely differing origins. Basically however the immediate cause is confusion and conflict resulting from the clash of powerful forces,.. the genetics of evolution against the environment of society. In other words nature against nurture. Let us consider them separately,.. nurture first.

Most of today's senior adults were raised in a rather strict and restricted society. They followed several similar generations and they passed on the tradition to the younger generation. A major influence is religion, a strictly adhered to and practised way of life. Though hypocrisy was common,.. little children of seven or eight years old worked in coal mines, and women had no legal rights,.. the moral requirements of religion were obeyed. The interpretation of religion was that sex was somehow wrong and dirty,.. though there is little in the fundamental religions teachings of Christ or Muhammad to suggest so. It was the followers-on of the true religious leaders who produced the unpleasant associations. Adultery was frowned on with good cause; it broke the rules of possession and destroyed a man certainty that the offspring that would inherit his name and property were really his. Here and there too there are hints that promiscuous sex was unacceptable.

Nowhere however is good, strenuous, enjoyable and varied sex between two devoted partners forbidden. Nevertheless, once in control, people retain control by producing rules and laws and ensuring that others obey. So it was with religion and politics. Rules about sex became adopted as part of the life-style of society.

Teachers and thinkers of all kinds saw the disadvantages of indiscriminate sex,.. the transmission of disease, unwanted pregnancies, illegitimacy, illegal abortions, ruined lives and marriages and the general threat to society. Gradually all this became exaggerated to the extent that in the society of the Twenties, Thirties and Forties, when most seniors were growing up, everything to do with sex was a furtive, unrespectable business. Sex could not be talked about. Education in sexual matters was unthinkable. Exposure of the body, especially its 'private parts', was impossible even between husband and wife in many cases. Masturbation was held to be a dangerous product of a sick mind. Sex was a thoroughly nasty, dirty, foul and unspeakable business. The bare essentials required to ensure pregnancy were the most that could be tolerated.

Punishments were severe. To be caught masturbating meant at least a thrashing. To lose virginity meant ostracism. An illegitimate pregnancy could mean being sent away from home, family and community. No-one of sexual reputation was esteemed in society. Children were taught that sex was wicked, and they were forbidden to know anything or to try anything. The years of ignorant childhood lengthened into the years of frustrated adolescence and eventually into the years of inhibited adulthood. The grip of the 'Thou Shalt Not' Brigade was secure. Few grew up without the conviction that sex was disgusting,.. even if it was nice. Few grew up without guilts that they had sexual thoughts, and fears as to the retribution that they could bring. As a whole, society was a mass of deliberate ignorance, shameful education and a never ending threat of guilt, remorse and punishment,.. a long tradition in Judaeo-Christian religious groups.

Against this seemingly immovable, man-made object,.. this immensely powerful armour of society's appalling methods of upbringing,.. came crashing, head on, the irresistible, older and stronger force of nature. The clash was colossal.

The Rules of Nature

It is a basic function of living things that they reproduce. Nothing is more important in the very nature of things than that creatures of all kinds survive to breed. As it is so ultimately important it comes as no surprise that the impulse to breed, the sheer drive to accomplish procreation, is of unequalled power. It cannot and will not be safely thwarted. Love, they say, will find a way. That is possible. That sex most assuredly will is certain. And sex is the chosen vehicle of human reproduction.

The urge to find a mate, indeed as many mates as possible, is an inclination patterned indelibly into the genes. If cats are segregated from all other cats from the instant of birth, they will still respond without any experience or learning. When the young, untaught females come into season they will nevertheless still stand ready to receive servicing.

When the young males catch the female season-odour they will nevertheless still fight amongst themselves in order to provide that servicing. For a short while everything,.. associates, surroundings, even food and water requirements, will be forgotten. Sex alone is what counts.

In humans the picture is little different. The sexual urge, left to nature, is irresistible. Furthermore, humans, with their ability of thought, learning and passing on information, have developed the potentials of sex. For them there are no seasons, though sexual desires do periodically vary in intensity. For them the sexually attractive features of the opposite sex are frequently flaunted or at any rate have attention drawn to them,.. the medallion suspended on the brawny chest, the moustache and beard of the male,.. the rouged female lips, partly exposed bosom or exaggerated 'bustle' of different eras are all such examples.

Man has opened up most of his vital needs to variation and exploitation. He wears not only the essential protection of simple clothing but a mass of fashionable extras some of them deliberately sexual. He has widened the scope of his needs for food and drink to include the entire world variety of tastes and aromas and the enormous range of differently flavoured beverages. And in sex has been developed the great diversity of sexual positions, fantasies, deviations and perversions.

These then are the nature of the clashing giants,.. the natural overwhelming urge and guidance towards lots of sex on the one hand and, on the other, the restrictive, repressive prohibitions of upbringing which despite their unnatural qualities are profoundly ingrained into the developing psyche of the infant.

The result in the majority of instances is an adult that behaves like a football between opposing teams, kicked hither and thither and never settling. Perhaps a better simile is the adventurous animal on an elastic leash,.. constantly striving to move towards its natural ends, yet endlessly yanked back by the man-made tether around its neck.

In the grown person an uneasy balance is usually the best that can be reached. Sex is needed, desired and sought, but secretly and fearfully. Sex is found and enjoyed in limited quantities but guiltily and with subsequent remorse. (Revealingly there is the apocryphal joke about the recently made Jewish pornographic movie which consisted of five minutes of sex,.. and two hours of remorse!)

Sexual failure

In this fertile bed of utter confusion germinate the seeds of misery that will flower as impotence and female frigidity or anorgasmia. The ability to relish sex and indulge in it as wholeheartedly as all other creatures has been crippled by bungling philosophy and blundering education,.. and sometimes deliberately at that. The complex resultant of sex urge competing with inhibitions produces a life-long unresolved conflict. People who indulge in sex, and somehow or other most do, are frequently troubled by uncertainties, anxieties and guilts.

There is the further complication of fear. It operates in women but even more so in men,.. the fear of failure. Major aspects of the appeal of a man to a woman are his size, his power, his success. If he is of small stature in any of these he feels insecure and diminished. If he fails,.. if that failure to perform and impress takes place in the bedroom, it is the worst humiliation of all.

This creates the inexorable vicious circle or rather spiral, for it not only continues but worsens. Here again is a partial list, this time of the psychogenic and organic-psychogenic causes of impotence. And once again, though incomplete, it is a formidable list:-

Organic:

Depression and other forms of psychopathology
Stress from job or status concerns
Guilt for whatever reason including extramarital affairs or loss of interest in the spouse
Hostility toward the spouse
Underconfidence
Feelings of inadequacy
Shame of body or fantasies
Performance anxiety
Fatigue
Religious constraints

Organic/psychogenic causes:

Normal ageing process
Chronic diseases such as diabetes or anaemia
Painful urination/Frequent urination at night
Rectal pain or low abdominal pain

Stress incontinence
Insomnia/Chronic fatigue
Malnutrition

A shred of hope

Summarising the entire causality of impotence we can say this,.. impotence is predisposed to by a combination of cultural inhibitions, ignorance, poor communication and certain physical conditions. It is actually initiated by a combination of physical and emotional causes including past experiences and a concern for any partner's problems. It is perpetuated by such things as the partner's pressure on the man to perform, criticism and ridicule, denial or even expressions of patronising sympathy. It is also perpetuated by the individual's own loss of confidence, guilt, shame, performance anxieties, frustrations and anger.

These act intermittently along the path of failure, leading to fear of further failure, leading in turn to the actual positive expectation of further failure, and leading eventually and almost certainly to repeated failure itself. The disastrous, self-replicating sequence is securely established.

* * *

After that almost demoralising and seemingly inescapable series of available disasters it is as well to restate the counterbalance. There are many and varied and highly successful therapies now available for impotence. They will shortly be described. The difficulty is that for many they are rather slow and tiresome to use. They are also hard to find and in some cases too costly to be within everyone's reach. Simpler, inexpensive, D-I-Y techniques, like the Miracle Method, are well worth a try first. Speak to your doctor. Tell him your intention. And if he has no objection, what is there to be lost?

* * *

Chapter Three

SELF-ASSESSMENT AND SELF-HELP

In spite of the official response of society, which is disapproval of the randy, promiscuous man, in secret he is in fact actually regarded as rather an admirable fellow. Conversely, the randy woman,.. the 'fallen' woman of society, is never esteemed socially. She is however, covertly welcomed by men, albeit cautiously and invariably envied by women, albeit secretly.

The cuckolded man, on the other hand, is an object of ridicule, as also, or even more so, is the impotent man. Each is regarded as a fit subject for jokes, sympathy perhaps, but certainly no great respect. Yet, as we have seen impotence is widespread and cuts across all segments of society. The simple farmworker, tormented by the guilts instilled by his strict religious upbringing, suffers just the same as the business tycoon who failed once with a call-girl when he was drunk and has gone in terror of further failure every day of his life since. So does that man who caught a mild gonorrhoea in a Hong Kong brothel, was quickly cured, but whose fear made him impotent for the next ten years. So does the man whose teenage sweetheart laughed at his small penis,.. the man who saw his wife of thirty years out with another man,.. the man afraid of another heart attack,.. the man whose wife goes to bed in curlers and a nightie that should have become a duster years ago.

Clinics in Zululand report that those huge, black warriors get impotence. So did Genghis Khan,.. and the poet Goethe; so did Red Indian braves, so do macho, Spanish studs and the virile Polynesians of the South Pacific. So do Australian crocodile hunters, scuba divers and parachutists. And so do accountants, bank clerks and insurance salesmen.

Our society is no different. It is riddled with erectile difficulties at every level. So rest assured, if you are suffering the agonies of impotence, you are not alone. Everywhere the problem is on the increase, affecting more and more men,.. and their partners.

The major difference for you, the reader, is that you and your partner have access to private, at-home treatment right here in this guide to the Twenty Minute Method.

Knowing yourself

Before embarking on the programme itself, the first stage is self-assessment. Ask yourself these questions:-

1. When did the problem begin?
2. Has the problem been continuous or are there times when it is infrequent?
3. Has the problem been worsening?
4. Have you been under stress or anxiety concerning your work, finances, marriage or relationship during this time?
5. Did the problem coincide with an illness or did it show itself after treatment of an illness?
6. Has your consumption of alcohol increased during this period?
7. Are you taking drugs, either medicinal or recreational, that you had not been using before the problem?

For the next few weeks, even as you enjoy improvement from other methods in this book, carefully examine your life-style for common erection saboteurs. It would pay you handsomely too to get some more detailed background on sex and your sexual equipment. Read the books 'The Penis' and 'Age and Sex' (See Sources List at the end of this book). Both will give you and your partner enormous amounts of useful data, ideas and perhaps rather shocking suggestions.

You already know that prescription medicines may be at the root of your problem. But, did you ever stop to think that it could be your cigarette smoking? Surprisingly, some men find that if they stop smoking their erections return in a flash. Smoking destroys potency by constricting blood vessels, including those in the penis that are essential to building erections. The result of cigarettes is that not enough blood may be able to get into the penis to produce or maintain an erection. Some men discover that soon after they give up smoking their ability to have intercourse returns as the blood vessels regain their ability to hold blood. (Please note: tobacco is the culprit, which means that chewing tobacco, nicotine-filled gum and other similar products can also have similar deleterious effects on your erections.)

If the thought of quitting tobacco forever is too overwhelming, try quitting for three short weeks. That amount of time without nicotine should be enough to let you know if eliminating tobacco will help or even cure your impotence problem. Furthermore after that trial three weeks you'll probably decide to quit anyway,.. and you'll have proved that you can.

Another substance you should cut down on is alcohol. You need not give it up entirely, but you should drink only moderately, especially if you have been a heavy or regular drinker. Too much alcohol can ruin potency in the short run. And in the long run, too much alcohol can diminish the size of a man's testicles, decrease sexual desire, and render him impotent. No more than the equivalent of between one half and one bottle of white table wine per day is the maximum permitted ration.

Contrary to popular belief, alcohol does not reduce inhibitions in the anxious or uptight male. Only if a man is totally relaxed, secure and able to concentrate on sex, may alcohol help him respond sexually and enjoy a different kind of sexual experience. So, reducing alcohol especially prior to sex may help you determine if alcohol is the culprit in your potency problem.

While you're searching for potency causes, this is a reminder to consult your doctor about those prescription medicines. However, never reduce, eliminate or change the way you take prescribed drugs without first checking with your physician. Don't tamper with medication under any conditions.

Chances are high that these few simple measures of

1. Quitting smoking.
2. Decreasing alcohol.
3. Checking your medicines

may eliminate your potency problems. If so, congratulations,.. you are one of about 30% of all impotent men who need only make these few easy adjustments to renew their virility. But, if this isn't the case for you, let's move on to the next set of guidelines for finding a cure.

By the way, no matter what your potency problems are, or aren't, the chapter coming up on Sexual Therapy at Home will be of great therapeutic benefit,.. and pleasurable interest to you.

Emotional causes

Now, let's try to identify that 20% to 40% of all men who suffer from psychogenic impotence. If all the points below are true about you, your impotence probably does not have a physical cause:-

1. You are in good health.
2. You are not currently taking any kind of medications.
3. You do not now, nor have you ever, regularly abused alcohol or drugs.
4. You have never suffered a trauma, injury or disease of the pelvic area or nervous system.
5. You experience real morning erections, or, when you wake up you sometimes find that your penis is at least partly rigid.
6. You are able to masturbate and achieve a firm, maintainable erection.
7. You have the same level of sexual desire as before you became impotent.

Did you answer "YES" to all these descriptions? Now, do you answer "YES" to any one of the following:-

1. You recently changed jobs.
2. You are very worried about your finances.
3. Your level of stress has increased.
4. You avoid physical intimacy with your wife.
5. There has been a recent death within your immediate family.
6. You have been dieting strenuously.
7. You have recently moved your home or job.
8. You are overdue for a holiday.

If any of the above circumstances applied to you, stress or general anxiety may be slowing down your sex life. If so, why not give yourself a break from worrying about your erection problem. Sometimes, the best way to start having good sex is to stop having any kind of sex at all,.. for a time.

The following chapter offers an 'intimacy rediscovery' programme that is for all men, but it is especially effective for men suffering from psychogenic impotence. If your sexual problem does not have a physical cause, the following could straighten everything out for you. So, just relax, be patient, and learn how you can become your own sexual therapist!

* * *

Chapter Four

SEX THERAPY AT HOME

Everything that has gone before in this book boils down to one bottom-line statement,.. if you are impotent you can't have sex. Isn't that right?

No! It isn't.

Your impotence may be temporarily stopping you altogether. It may just be curtailing you. You may have the kind of relationship where you get a glow just from pleasuring your partner by masturbating her or giving her oral sex without actually getting any of the real thing yourself. It may have forced you to retreat into a fantasy sex world where the best you can do is dream about past pleasures and imagine future ones.

But none of these things automatically mean that you really and truly can't have sex. Its more a question of what kind of sex,.. and when. For, as a matter of fact, it is possible to conquer the heart-break of impotence well within half an hour. That will all be completely explained when we get to the Twenty Minute Method. First though, in the interest of making this a thorough and comprehensive guide to impotence management, let us consider the other methods of treatment and their success rates which range from disappointing to very good indeed.

Early difficulties

Until the sixties impotence was a subject rarely discussed,... in common with most sexual subjects. Only gradually did the medical profession start to take note and try to help. Treatments were poor and poorly understood. Quacks abounded in the field,... as they still do. All over the world, right into the central bastion of medicine, Harley Street in London, unqualified tricksters and charlatans peddled, and are still peddling their worthless trash. To desperate men who would pay anything for the return of their sex lives, the con-men marketed an astonishing range of costly, ineffective rubbish.

A few things, like the Energising Ring, of which more later,.. did work but had to be sold secretly in order to avoid oppressive laws.

Only gradually did it become respectable for real doctors to take an interest in sexual subjects. Those involved were a frequent source of ridicule and experienced considerable professional ostracism. It is to their credit that they persevered.

In treating impotence the use of sexual surrogates or independent partners is sometimes recommended. It is a fact that many cases are what are called situational or responsive impotence. That is it is the actual situation,.. the home, the bedroom, the bed, which induce the impotence. Away from those, performance is better.

Alternatively, in responsive cases the man is impotent with only one woman, usually his wife. By undergoing training sessions in different environments by a skilled surrogate 'lover' a man can often break what is, in effect, a vicious spiral and then resume his chosen relationship successfully. Of course this method is costly, too costly for most. It may also require considerable moderation of instinctive responses of repulsion and jealousy on the part of the couple with the problem.

It is for these reasons that surrogacy is seldom utilised. However, it is worth pointing out that a man, more so in his later years, is prone to become impotent if his regular partner becomes unavailable for a while, for example during illness. It is well worth considering whether a temporary surrogate partner, objectionable though that idea may seem at first sight, may not prove a better long term choice than a seriously blighted sexual and therefore pair-bond relationship.

Different treatments

Nowadays there is an entire range of therapies available to the impotent male. An excellent range of books and booklets concerning sexual problems is published by an ethical group of experts in England (see Source List) The one covering impotence lists the various options available and suggests a programme of management right through from the simplest cases to the most severe. A couple could do no better than to follow the suggested routine.

When the case reaches the care of an expert physician one of the things he will require is a Nocturnal Penis Tumescence test. This test uses one of a number of small measuring devices to ascertain whether a man undergoes erection during his sleep and to what extent. The penis which is impotent for organic disease reasons seldom erects at night. The penis impotent for psychological reasons usually does. The test affords a method of diagnosis between the two types. There are surprises to be expected,.. both ways.

Where earlier, easier methods have failed the technique of injection may be tried. The technique is not difficult to learn but it does require an element of courage. An active substance is injected actually into the shaft of the penis shortly before intercourse is intended. Correctly done, in the majority of men the result is a worthwhile erection sufficient, to enable satisfactory penetration and which lasts for a long enough time, usually up to an hour or more. As experience is gained a man becomes able to judge the dosage with considerable accuracy in relation to the firmness required and the duration.

There have been some problems arising from over-frequent use of the method. Hardening and scarring of the penis has resulted in its unsightly projection under everyday clothing while in the non-erect state. Reduction in sensitivity too has affected some. In general however it remains an excellent technique for those prepared to adopt it.

Long-term impotence is more difficult to treat successfully by medical means. As a consequence in recent years a great deal of experimental work has been done on surgical therapies. These have revolved around the use of a prosthesis. This is a device usually made of silicone-rubber and which can be actually implanted within the penis. Under anaesthetic an incision is made either in the shaft of the penis, or near the abdominal wall or junction with the scrotum. A pair of rods are then slid directly into the tissue of the corpus cavernosum of the penis (there are two) on each side.

Basically there, are two varieties of protheses, one a solid semi-rigid rod the other an inflatable hollow rod. The solid rod is the simpler to insert and use. It is flexible to a degree but quite stiff enough to hold the penis erect for vaginal penetration. Its disadvantage is that during the rest of the time, when not in sexual use, the penis remains protruding inconveniently. This presents difficulties turning in bed during sleep and also means that the penis can only be positioned up against the abdominal wall under the normal clothing.

To overcome these inconveniences, the more complicated, inflatable types are used. Some are self-contained but most have a reservoir of inflation fluid inserted beneath the abdominal muscles. From this a tube runs down to a small pump placed inside the scrotum rather like an extra testicle. The pump is easily accessible without discomfort and with a few gently squeezes transfers fluid to the two implanted hollow rods. A simulated erection takes place and can be retained. When the need is over a release valve on the pump is activated, fluid returns to the reservoir, and the penis resumes its non-erect state.

Most couples find this latter a better method as erection seems more natural and the penis presents no social difficulties as a result of a permanent, partial rigidity. Complications are rare though infection usually means the prosthesis must be removed. Patients return to work as soon as the insertion wound is healed and intercourse can commence after four to six weeks.

The very precise nature of the prosthesis and the surgical skill needed to insert them comfortably makes them expensive. Except where they are paid for under health service schemes or insurances, they often prove beyond the reach of many. Alternative treatments however exist for long-term or short-term impotence sufferers which are, in this writer's opinion, every bit as good, far less costly, need no outside assistance and should most certainly be tried before expensive counselling or surgery are resorted to.

Erection mechanisms

These are erection aids and penis-training programmes. There are now several available with varying costs and complexities and varying success rates. They fall into two groups, those used to produce erection and which are then removed for intercourse, and those worn during intercourse.

The latter type, for example as marketed under the trade-name Correctaid, consists of a thick walled rubber condom. When this is in position on the flaccid penis a suction device withdraws air from between the two and encourages a useful degree of erection. This along with the stiffness of the condom permits penetration to take place. Clearly its disadvantages are that the degree of erection is rather limited and that the loss of sensation occasioned by the thick wall is seldom appreciated.

Other suction devices are also on the market under such trade names as Pos-T-Vac, ACTIVE, Erecaid and Response. These too depend on inserting the penis into a tube from which air is then drawn out with a pump. Once the penis is erected a constricting band around the base of the penis helps erection to be maintained. The pumps themselves are usually quite easy to use though the various sizes and adapters together with a vacuum gauge appear rather formidable to some. There is no doubt that these methods do work and they are gaining in popularity. The main drawback is that most are in a very high price bracket, up around £250 ($450), though ACTIVE, being simpler, is correspondingly less costly.

ACTIVE in particular deserves to be selected for a special mention. The entire concept was developed in Sweden, a country long-renowned for being in the very forefront of sexual-medical research. In that country there are no restrictions on the open discussion and publication of sexual matters as, very wisely, they the Swedes were amongst the first to divest themselves of the idiotic censorship laws that beset England and America. It was thus fairly easy for researchers not only to work in the field of sexual problems but actually to secure government aid in combating the serious effects of disturbed sexuality on individuals and the nation alike. The organisation RFSU was established with government sponsorship and funding to correlate various aspects of sex in relation to the the population. Amongst a vast amount of helpful literature and inexpensive counselling and therapeutic clinics, they have also produced, experimented with and tested various kinds of sexually-assistant devices. One of these is ACTIVE. Its principles are the same as most,.. an erection pump and the resulting erection retained by a constrictive circlet. But the simplicity, quality and ingenuity with which it has been designed and produced make it a head and shoulders winner in the opinion of the present writer. Combined with such low cost its success rate make it well worth consideration by all serious sufferers from impotence. (See Sources List.)

Similarly recommended is the Penatone Programme and its advanced continuation programme, Maxitone. Elsewhere in this book is also described the 'Energising Ring' and its erection ability and erection-sustaining capacities. It is mentioned here again as its value in conjunction with the Penatone Programme has proved so considerable,.. as too has

Masculone, also explained elsewhere.

Used in combination these methods,.. Penatone, Masculone, Active and the Ring,.. have probably contributed more to the entire question of impotence therapy, penis training,.. and both male and female pride and satisfaction, than any other medical technique known to this writer.

Do-It-Yourself treatment

We come now, at last, to the sexual re-training programme that embodies the Miracle Method. It is possible to skip the first stage which takes longer and needs more effort. Plenty of men go straight into the second stage and do very well indeed. But properly kept statistics show clearly that the best successes by the largest numbers of men come from those who do both stages really thoroughly.

Let's begin with the basics. If the loss of sexual ability has you in its grip, it is well known that the very best way to break the vicious circle is to have sex. So, what do you do? Why, you go ahead and have sex. But how, you ask? We'll show you how right here.

Absolutely and without doubt sexual intercourse with real penile penetration is what beating impotence is all about. Sexual rejuvenation begins with the confidence, the certain knowledge, that you can have sex on demand,.. good sex, any time and every time. It was for that purpose that the Twenty Minute Method was developed,.. because nothing succeeds like success. It guarantees sexual intercourse for impotent men. It ensures that you can have sex,.. real sex,.. the kind of good, wholesome sex you've been missing, immediately.

All you need for the method is a penis and a partner. Given those two it is possible to promise that you can once again share the thrill of being inside your partner within twenty minutes and no matter how severe your sexual problem is.

Remember, you can have sex. You will have sex again. Thousands have used The Miracle Method before you. Some of those were men whose organs had remained limp and useless despite their partners' most strenuous efforts to offer intense stimulation,.. men who could not erect, or enter, or ejaculate,.. men who felt they had too small a penis,.. who only dribbled a little semen at orgasm,.. men who were impotent due to disease, injury, stress or medication,.. men who were getting on in years. Yet, for each of these men, life changed. They took the steps to remedy their sagging sexuality. They discovered that sexual penetration could again become an immediate reality.

After a careful follow-up of these patients, for as much as ten years in some cases, it was revealed that the majority never went back to the limp and disheartening experiences of the past,.. and those who from time to time did have later recurrences, the Method worked again just as well as before.

So, now to the Method itself.

* * *

THE TWENTY MINUTE MIRACLE METHOD... an impotence correction programme for men

Stage One.

Although the second stage of this programme takes a mere twenty minutes, Stage One takes longer. Although Stage One can be leap-frogged, it is good but defiantly not nearly as good to go straight to Stage Two. Although Stage Two guarantees the short cut of immediate penis into vagina penetration, it is Stage One that prepares the ground,.. and vastly reduces the chances of failure or of later recurrence.

So be advised,.. even though Stage One, the stage of Intimacy Rediscovery, takes about ten weeks. Those ten weeks may turn out to be the most interesting and rewarding weeks of your life.

Whatever stage of sexual development you are in, however experienced a lover, however 'good in the sack', you got that way through training and practice. You acquired your skills. You were not born with them. You were born with the sexual equipment and the sexual urge to use it. You had to learn the pleasures, the subtleties, the techniques. In other words you went through years, in all probability, of training to get where you are. And now that training has let you down. Something has gone wrong. The correct sequence has been broken. It should be a sequence of:- desire-arousal-erection-penetration-ejaculation.

It must be re-established.

Let us assume that the reason for your impotence is due at least in part, to emotional and psychological factors. It's a pretty safe assumption as most men do fall into this category. Knowing that sexual problems can be thus traced back to emotional problems inspired sexual medicine experts and therapists to develop a re-learning system. It is identical in principle with the re-structuring programmes that are now used throughout various aspects of medicine, from teaching an amputee to walk and work again, to overcoming the effects of regional paralysis, to eliminating serious emotional problems and resuming healthy activities. In this specialised programme you actually rediscover and re-learn sexual pleasures, focusing on different aspects over the training period. Then, gradually, the whole series of your own personal sexual responses and reflexes becomes re-conditioned. This systematic refocusing of sensations and responses with one chosen and co-operative partner is what is nowadays termed Intimacy Re-discovery.

It all takes time,.. the human body and brain do not adapt trivially in seconds but thoroughly over weeks. But the entire programme really does work,.. extremely well. That has been proven in many parts of the world, and over and over again. It can work for you too if you give it a proper chance. Don't be misled into thinking its all psychobabble,.. a lot of high-falutin small-talk. It isn't. It is a well-planned and carefully designed, very successful technique that is in use from one end of the world to the other. Give it the opportunity to work for you, eh? What have you got to lose?

If your partner has not yet read this book it is high time she did. As with many projects in life, it is teamwork that pays off. And as with many projects in a relationship, most of the credit for success belongs to the woman. This was never more true than in the successful combating of impotence. When that limp response and emasculated image has left you,.. when, once again, you feel like a two-fisted, red-blooded, broad-shouldered, hairy-chested man full of vigour and virility,.. when all that happens, as it will, remember to show your gratitude to she who made it possible.

And a warning to womenfolk. Your man is in trouble,.. deep trouble. If you do not help him, if you are reluctant and supercilious instead of wholehearted and enthusiastic then you can never earn,.. or deserve, his ultimate admiration and devotion. Read this book, or at least the following section. And if you really want to seize this opportunity fully, read Chapter Five, called 'A Word To Her'. It will shock you, disgust you perhaps. But it will enlighten you too if you let it,.. and it will open a few interesting doors to a brighter future for you too.

Sex temporarily abandoned

When you, as an impotence sufferer, embark upon the intimacy re-discovery routine, the very first thing you do is to stop having sex. From day one of week one on to the last day of week ten, full sexual intercourse is totally banned. This in itself comes as a relief to some men. The pressure to do it, to perform, to try, to face the same old humiliation is lifted,.. gone. Chances are it will never return, not as a pressure or a duty anyway. From now on it will all be a pleasure.

But, and this is vital,.. from this moment on, until the programme is completed, sexual intercourse is utterly forbidden. There will certainly be moments when you feel so good, and your response feels so good, that you will be tempted to throw caution to the winds and go for it,.. to lay that co-operative partner back onto the bed and penetrate her welcoming body.

Don't do it!

Be warned. That is not a short cut to success. It is a turn-off along the road to disaster. Your partner should remember too, that it is wrong to make this mistake. She should be ready to help you resist, even if she wants you badly and feels in her heart that you could make it. Sex is prohibited,.. off limits,.. out of bounds. Obey the rules! They are there for you.

If you attempt intercourse during the ten weeks preliminary training,.. you are doomed to trouble. It cannot be too heavily stressed that just for those weeks

REAL SEX IS OUT!

After that you can soon make up for lost time with a vengeance!!

During the week by week programme you and your partner will become involved in a progressive and deeply intimate form of physical contact exploring and re-exploring each others bodies in the most deliberate and thorough manner. This will give enjoyable time, but also time for locating doubts, hesitations and embarrassments. And it will give time for the self-assessment of pleasures and for a confident mutual communication level to develop. It will reveal areas of ignorance and bring to the surface any deep-seated taboos or myths about sexuality. It operates equally well in these aspects for both partners. When problems arise they are discussed frankly and either overcome or an easy comfortable temporary compromise achieved. There is no sense of fear or hostility or humiliating submission involved. Everything is seen and done with the aim of improving the performance of both partners, their co-operation levels, and above all, the lasting strength of their relationship.

The programme goes like this:-

WEEK ONE:

Week One is taken up with what is termed General Pleasuring. It is a tender and beautiful activity which goes back to the primary contact moves of a commencing relationship. All you do is to caress each other, but in a way that will increase sexual awareness while minimising sexual activity. Go through the following exercises every day. Usually the evening after a relaxing shower is the best time. You are going to take turns in the manoeuvre so decide in advance which of you is to be caressed first, and which the caresser. For example, if you as the man have felt pressured or guilty in your sexual relationship or if you have potency problems, you should probably caress your partner first. On the other hand if you sense that your partner is inhibited or shy, then perhaps she should caress you first.

Don't get all coy and self-conscious. Don't make the mistake,.. and it is a mistake, of thinking this part of the routine is a bit silly. If you do it is probably only due to your own sense of shyness,.. which, in turn, is a sign of underconfidence. Remember this whole programme is designed to alter all that. And it will if you give it full opportunity. This is not silly nonsense. It is a return to the fundamental and highly successful, natural, biological conditioned pathways of human beings. Stick with it,.. and give it everything you've got. Much is at stake.

So, after your shower, you should both remove all your clothes, and lie down or lounge on the bed or other comfortable area. Then the person who is the caress-receiver should lie face down in a relaxing position. The partner doing the caressing begins to caress, stroke and massage the other person as gently, lovingly and tenderly as possible. The caresser can stand, kneel over or sit alongside.

Start with the back of the head, the ears, the neck. Slowly move down the back and sides. Gently hold and massage the buttocks and the insides of the thighs. Tenderly, move on to the legs and feet. Do not approach or touch the genital area. Stroke the skin, gently knead the finger tips and knuckles into underlying muscles, lightly scrape finger nails over skin, curl fingers into the hair,.. anything.

The person who is the object of all this grooming love and touching should concentrate on his or her own feelings. It sounds a bit selfish, but it isn't really. In fact it is a very important part of the technique because, as mentioned earlier, the aim is to expand the pleasure pathways to the brain. There should be no concern on the part of the receiver as to whether or not the caress-giver is getting tired or bored. After all, you are taking turns. Thus, the received should try to stay with his or her feelings and also to talk to and give feedback to the caress-giver. If something feels unpleasant, the same is true. Don't wince or shout 'ouch' but rather explain that something else felt better or ask that that sort of trick be given a miss.

After about ten minutes, it's time for the receiver to turn over and be caressed on the front. Care is taken throughout to avoid touching or stimulating the genital areas. Again, spend about ten minutes on caressing the front. Then it's time to change positions. The caress-receiver becomes the caress-giver.

It is stressed once again that even though you may become sexually aroused, you must not proceed to have sexual intercourse. After your pleasuring session, you will probably feel pretty relaxed. You may feel like discussing the experience or you may want to fall asleep and save the discussion for later. Either reaction is allowed. If you want to get up and go about your business, you may do that also, but the suggestion is that you wait snugly lying side by side, perhaps holding hands, and just re....laxing, for an additional ten minutes. Don't be surprised if nothing happens. It is not supposed to be earth shattering or mind blowing,.. and it's early days yet, just you wait and see.

After seven days of this special technique, you will have become very much more conscious of your body,.. of what feels good, what is sexual arousing, and so on. You will probably also start to find yourself confronting certain sexual hang-ups. For example, if you didn't get an erection, you may have wondered "Why not?" Or, you may have said to yourself, "This is too much concentration on sex, I feel guilty," or simply "This is boring,.. is it worth it just for sex?" Don't be put off by, and don't ignore, these or other mildly unpleasant thoughts and feelings. They are important. They are all the tips of submerged icebergs. Let them surface. It will be useful for later on. But whatever you do don't worry about them or the lack of them. It will all come right. All such reactions, and others like them, are perfectly natural. Just put these thoughts aside, for now. We'll come back to your anxieties later.

Now, move on to the next week.

WEEK TWO:

This is devoted to experimenting with Genital Pleasuring.

Begin this exercise in exactly the same way as the previous exercise,.. with a shower and a comfortable place to recline fully nude. Just as before, there is a total ban on sexual intercourse and on orgasm,.. both remain absolutely forbidden for the time being.

The time span for this exercise is approximately twenty minutes per partner. This is the minimum time. You can take twice or three times as long if you wish, if you have the time, and if you enjoy it. The longer you practice the better.

To begin with, caress and stroke the entire body as in the first week. Use your fingers, hands, and now lips and body pressure too to encourage relaxation and a sensuous state of body and mind. A woman with long hair can also let it hang and brush over her partner. Once relaxation has begun, approach and start to concentrate on fondling the genitals. You can go to virtually any extreme of stimulation as long as you don't attempt intercourse or even allow orgasm. If things threaten to get a bit too close and out of control, back off immediately, or you will ruin everything.

One very important aspect of this exercise is to concentrate on and identify what feels good, and to show or tell your partner. Make a mental list of your favourite techniques and talk about it. You should also try to discover and develop new pleasure spots. Try some different techniques, give them a chance to feel good. Without doubt prolonged practice and repetition in sexual activities actually forge new neurological paths of pleasure to the brain. That is one of the things the brain does best. Let it do its job as nature intended.

You may find that you get an erection. If so, great. But just don't allow yourself to reach a climax. If you don't have an erection, don't worry about it. Just abandon yourself and your anxieties to the intimate pleasure and relaxation of the moment.

As the week progresses, you will find yourself becoming more sexually aware and more alive and interested in the pleasures of life. You will probably also be wondering when you can actually consummate the sex act. Fortunately, you will find that a little fulfilment is coming up in the next week.

WEEK THREE:

This is a pivotal week in developing your new sexuality. You will be allowed to experience sexual climax. But first, there are some important ground rules.

1. You still may not have intercourse under any conditions.
2. You must take turns,.. one day one partner is climaxed, the next day the other. On day seven, you both may have orgasms. Don't depart from this regime even if you both feel one partner needs to orgasm more than the other. No cheating allowed.
3. If you are still afflicted with impotence, you must accept genital and overall pleasuring for double the allocated twenty minute time span instead of climaxing.
4. Climaxing is not mandatory. If it does not happen, it's perfectly okay.

This week's exercises are designed to allow you to put your new found erotic techniques to use.

Begin in exactly the same way as the two previous weeks with a shower and a place to relax naked. The very routine in itself has become a relaxing reflex by this time. You should allow your partner to receive her pleasure first and climax first. Caress and fondle her until she relaxes and begins to feel aroused. Then, concentrate on stimulating her intimate zone with your hands, fingers, lips, anything. But do not enter her with your penis. If she likes a soft shaving brush on her nipples or a moist fingertip on her clitoris,.. fine. Anything goes. By using oral or manual techniques and with her giving suggestions or even giving herself additional self-stimulation, she should be able to reach a climax as long as she wants to. She is not obliged to achieve this, certainly not at the start or if she does not yet feel comfortable about it. There is no hurry. On the other hand she will be aware that for her partner to succeed in giving her an orgasm he can actually watch is very strong medicine for his condition.

The next day, change roles, but remember, still no intercourse.

On day seven, you will be engaging in mutual lovemaking. You may stroke, cuddle, caress, masturbate, lick, suck,.. anything. Both of you may climax, but you must do so without vaginal penetration.

During the week, it is vital to remember that climaxing is not mandatory. As you have learned previously, physical contact without climaxing can be very rewarding and loving. Perhaps you have certain anxieties that prevent you from functioning sexually just yet. But, even if your penis doesn't work for the time being, you should know by now that there are alternative sexual techniques and remedies. You know there is no pressure on you or on the time when you will become successful. There is absolutely no hurry. Time is on your side. You can be sure too that by now fresh and stronger nerve pathways to the brain's pleasure centres are well on the way to becoming established. Things are happening although you can't yet see them. And better is to come.

WEEK FOUR:

During the prior weeks, you may have met with ultimate success or you may be a shade disappointed in your attempts to rediscover your sexual self. For most people, the results of this programme fall somewhere between the two extremes. Therefore, you may have some problems, questions or anxieties that you would like to resolve. So, for this entire week, you may not engage in any form of sexual activity. Get that quite straight,.. no sex at all,.. not fondling or sucking or stroking or anything. Instead, you must spend your special evening training period with your partner,.. talking and reading.

First it is recommended that you purchase some good reading material on the subject of sex. There are some suggestions for you in the Sources List in the back of this book. But even reading this book, especially parts like 'A Word to Her' and the questions lists in Chapter Three, will provide plenty of talk-over material. In the evenings of this week, you should shower and become nude as other evenings and go to bed or sit comfortably in privacy with your partner. To open the lines of communications, we suggest that you ask each other the following questions.

1. What have you learned about your own body?
2. What did you learn about your partner's body?
3. What didn't you like,.. and why didn't you like it?
4. What did you think about while your partner was pleasuring you? Pleasure? Performance anxiety? Your work? Erotic fantasies? Why?
5. If you had problems climaxing, why do you think this happened?
6. Were you satisfied and happy even if you didn't climax? Why?
7. What do you like about your sexual relationship? What would you like to change?
8. What would you like him or her to do to you or with you?

Of course questions such as these must be answered honestly. What's more, if the answers offend you, and they may well at this stage, you should say so. For example, "I appreciate your frankness, but I feel hurt because,.. " It is vital to get such deep feelings to the surface so that both you can recognise them and your partner can learn about them. This is a very important stage in establishing knowledge and communication. Accept the faithful promise that it will lead on, past the doubts and the temporary hurt and build a vast new confidence. Instead of doubts you will have knowledge. Instead of hit and miss guessing you will know what is best,.. for both of you.

As you lie there naked and vulnerable, you will be learning a great deal about your sexuality and that of your partner. You may also become aroused, but you still must not have sex at all this week. Sex and discussions or criticisms of sex don't mix well with each other and can lead to inhibitions later on. Keep holding off. Sex of all kinds remains forbidden this week.

At this point, the problem of impotence may come up in your conversation. If you have this problem this next section is especially for you. But even if you are just doing this course for practice or as a prevention rather than a cure, it is a most useful section to study.

WEEK FIVE:

Nearly all men have problems achieving or maintaining an erection at some point in their lives. It's a normal event. Unfortunately, some men are so horrified when this happens that their anxiety over their potency inhibits the next erection and then the next.

During this week, if you've ever experienced problems with potency, it is recommended that you follow this technique especially carefully. If you are not worried about potency, this week will still bring to a culmination all that you have learned in previous weeks concerning sexual re-sensitisation.

First of all, you and your partner must recognise that this is your week, (that is, the man's), and your week in every respect.

You both are going to concentrate on the penis. In fact, this week is so fulfilling and exciting for most men that I've had male patients of mine lie to their wives and complain of potency problems just so they could get special attention and repeat the exercises in this week. That is a rotten trick of exploitation. Don't be so selfish,.. and foolish.

The strategy for maximising potency and reversing impotence where necessary is as follows:-

Step 1. Erotic enjoyment without erection.

Step 2. Erection without climax.

Step 3. Climax outside the vagina.

Step 4. Vaginal entry without climax.

Step 5. Vaginal entry and climax within.

To accomplish this, you must repeat the activities of Week One for the first night, thereby fulfilling Step 1. The next night is for Step 2; repeat the exercises of Week Two and allow yourself to have an erection. (Even if your penis remains very soft and there is nothing more than a sexual feeling in the penis, that is okay and qualifies as an erection.)

Step 3 will take place on the third night and means that you can climax outside the vagina. If you are able to climax, allow it to happen. Usually, this climax takes place as a result of masturbation or oral stimulation. But, whatever it is you need to have a climax, let it be known. Partners should co-operate at once, willingly and fully. No half-measures. By now, after all the sexual play and the deep sexual discussions the partner should know pretty near everything about the way he likes things best. So use them. After all you now have a lot of time invested in a very important procedure.

On the fourth night, the night after Step 3, do nothing at all of a sexual nature. But, the following night, put Step 4 into action, i.e. entry into the female without ejaculation.

At this point it is hoped that even impotent men are experiencing full-bodied erections, but if not, there is a technique that can ensure sexual penetration for you. That is the Twenty Minute Miracle Method, and in the next section you will learn its secret.

When you are ready, enter the female with your erection or by the Twenty Minute Method for non-erect penises described in the next chapter. Concentrate on your own pleasure. Use fantasy images if you like. Continue engaging in the movements of intercourse, but take it easy. Don't rush. Try to keep movements slow and controlled. The aim, if possible, is to enjoy the intercourse, but not to ejaculate. It is doesn't matter the least bit if you get carried away and simply overflow a great big climax. Nevertheless, if you can achieve this stage of intercourse without ejaculation, just this once, it adds a further impetus to the training routine,.. and it teaches you a measure of control and the fact that you can exercise that control. It is excellent training.

The next night or two are final success nights. Again you enter the vagina, either with your own erection or by the Twenty Minute Method. And this time you carry on with intercourse until you have either both had sufficient or until you ejaculate. Remember that on this occasion it is your pleasure that is the primary goal. Your partner is there to please you. To co-operate in any way you need. In short, to be used,.. and to be used for her man's pleasure,.. your pleasure. She must agree to this in advance or the entire point is lost.

Being so used is not a humiliating degradation but a mark of mutual and fundamental respect. It doesn't matter whether he wants her to be naked, or dressed up, or tied down,.. to give him oral sex,.. or whatever. She must go along. No reluctance or reticence. Very much it now all depends on her. She should have set out on the entire programme by being determined to use every trick she has learned to bring him on. She will know the kind of clothes he likes her to wear,.. high heels, a shorty-nightie, black mesh stockings? She will know the parts of him that respond best to touch by stroking or squeezing. She will know how and where and when he likes to give or receive oral sex. She will know how he likes to see her,.. walking around showing off her curves, lying demurely, rolling over face down, opening herself and exposing herself lewdly. She will know his favourite timing and his favourite positions for intercourse.

Now she uses all that knowledge and skill. It is in her hands, quite literally, to make the whole thing succeed.

For the majority of men, this exercise is extremely successful. By gradually breaking down the barriers of stress and anxiety, a man may recover full potency. Also, the repetition of the focusing exercise really does enable the brain to learn new ways of experiencing pleasure.

WEEKS SIX to TEN:

At this point in your program the best thing to do is to start all over again right back at the beginning of Week One. This is so even for those nearly fifty per cent of men who will by this time have had successful erections. "Why,.. ?" you may say to yourself. "Why should I do all this again when I've been so successful with my erection?"

The answer is that therapists all over the world have found that oftentimes success causes anxiety. "Will I be able to keep it up?" "Will my life change?" and so on. Therefore, it is only wise and healthy to begin again at Week One. Should any emotional problems or questions have developed, the second few weeks should resolve them. Indeed the more that your new relaxed pathways are repeated, the stronger and more resistant they are to any assaults that may be made on them ever again in the future. Repeating the course twice increases the success rates from about forty nine per cent up to nearly seventy per cent. A further course and the figure becomes eighty two per cent and a fourth course brings it to almost ninety per cent.

However, once you have completed the entire ten week programme, you'll understand on the most intimate levels how to arouse yourself and your partner to climax. In the future, should you ever have problems or feel that your sex life has slowed down, simply come back to these exercises and enjoy them once more. They comprise a technique that will work over and over again,... if you need it to.

And now, the Twenty Minute Miracle Method for Men,.. at last!

Countdown to success

Depending upon how many times you have repeated the weeks one to five training and re-training routines, you will by now have a very good chance of already having good erections! If not,.. never mind,.. you will. But this is important,.. even if your erections are already satisfactory it is a very good idea for you and your partner to practice the Twenty Minute Method. You never know when you might be glad of it. It is also another new technique learned. It is a first rate example of the combined effort at success of a couple devoted to each other. And, finally, most folk find it rather fun.

So, the advice is, whether you feel you need it or not,... do it anyway.

The Twenty Minute Miracle Method is not a major aphrodisiac pill or newly discovered super-scientific medicine. In fact, the dramatic results you'll find with this method have been used in sexual therapy clinics and recommended by doctors in the know, for a number of years.

This remarkable technique relies on human anatomy and physiology to allow the man to enter the woman with a semi-soft or even a completely soft penis. The very act of getting the penis, even when soft, actually into the vagina can often solve the potency problem. You can believe that implicitly for it is now a thoroughly proven fact. And it can be done. It was no idle promise that was made earlier. Sexual penetration is possible,.. and enjoyable.

Just feeling the penis in position and realising it is both possible to get it in soft, and pleasant when it's there, to some men, is so reassuring that normal erection resumes very quickly. All it amounts to is finding a position for sexual intercourse where the soft penis can enter the vagina.

In this case the essential is a patient and helpful partner. The best position is with the man on his back on a hard bed, or on the floor, and with pillow under his hips. The woman naked, crouches or squats, (kneeling is not as satisfactory as there is less control of angle and height) astride his waist and lowers herself down as if for ordinary intercourse in the woman-on-top position. As she gets down onto him she holds her vaginal lips well apart and at the same time, drawn backwards. This cannot be done properly with her hands in front. Her arms must go around the sides of her thighs and approach her vagina from the sides and rather from the back. Pulling the vaginal lips gently back as well as apart not only separates them but straightens the vaginal cavity so that its orifice will actually open. It is the way an examining physician starts his inspection. In fact, by using this method, it is possible to shine a torch up the vagina and even to treat certain problems there without need for unpleasant instruments. (Note to her: Try doing it over a mirror on the bathroom floor and you'll see that it really does work).

The man meanwhile supports his penis by drawing back the skin on the top and side of the penis root (in the pubic hair) and up into the gap beneath the pubic bones using both hands. Try this pulling up while at the same time applying a little pressure on both sides of the penis root with the finger tips. You will find it has the effect of producing a slight but definitely usable erection. This action constricts the veins and further improves the partial erection as the penis is raised and pointed. It really does work. Try it in private first and you will see. Some men find there are other useful tricks at this point, particularly that of using the Energising Ring. Details of this are given in Chapter Six: The Magical Extras.

In this way and with some suitable lubricant the soft penis will enter the widely opened vagina. As the soft head enters the first part of her orifice the woman now presses down firmly to prevent it slipping out. It will be felt to move further in. Movement can be only limited to start with, but with practice it really is effective, and very frequently a partial or complete erection will take place while the penis is already well inside the vagina. The actual surrounding pressure from the muscles of the vaginal orifice further constricts the penis and retains its blood. Added to the erotic sensations and to the appearance of the naked partner squatting over him these also contribute measurably to the erection potential.

The beauty of this unique penetration method is that it will work for nearly 100% of all men, even men with these problems:

overweight, obesity
high blood pressure
angina pectoris
prostate problems
pernicious anaemia
heart disease
emphysema
organic impotence
myocardial infarction
diverticulitis

alcoholism
hepatitis
hypothyroidism
diabetes
arthritis
cirrhosis
hip replacement
colitis,.. and many, many more conditions once thought of as erection-curtailing or restrictive of the more usual and strenuous forms of sexual intercourse.

All you need is a penis, a partner and this Twenty-Minute Miracle Method.

Let us create an imaginary sexual scenario so that you can see that this method can be virtually as romantic and fulfilling as sex with an already erect penis,.. as indeed it can according to very many users.

8.00 p.m. A romantic evening begins. You and your partner start the programme with the sensual techniques in the preceding chapter. By now you know how to arouse each other fully.

8.05 p.m. Prepare your partner for sexual entry by caressing what you have both learned are her most sexually sensitive areas. It is helpful to have her vaginal opening fully lubricated. Use a lubricant such as Nivea Cream, or a good quality body lotion,.. Oil of Ulay works very well, if necessary.

8.10 p.m. Penetration and insertion are guaranteed as your partner positions herself astride you and you guide your penis up into her vagina. Mutual caressing should continue at this stage, she stroking your face, chest and armpits, and you her breasts, nipples, ears and neck,.. and so on.

8.15 p.m. Gently begin the slight rocking pelvic movements of sexual intercourse. She slides a little back and forth upon you stimulating both your penis and her own clitoris. At the same time you push up with your pelvis, straining the penis up into her. These movements are natural and are designed, by nature, to increase penis blood flow and erection. Use whatever sexual fantasies and manual techniques that keep the mood one of highly exciting arousal. Continue sexual movements of intercourse through to climax and/or fulfilment.

Even though your penis may not become fully erect, it is possible for you to ejaculate. Also, by paying attention to your partner's needs and preferences, you can help her achieve climax too. This can be either while she is still astride and virtually masturbating herself on your genitals and pubic hair, or afterwards when she gets off and seeks (she should be offered it) some other form of satisfaction with fingers or tongue or vibrator.

The whole point of this method is to help you enjoy the ecstasy of sexual intimacy whether you have an erection or not. And you can. Be sure of it. Once you try this method, you'll find, much to your surprise probably, that great sex does not depend on your erection. You can succeed with any woman you desire and you can certainly experience the power of manly confidence just by taking command of the sexual situation.

Believe it too that your partner can have just as erotic and fulfilling a sexual experience through this method,.. if you both allow it to happen. What many men fail to understand is that sex is a total mind and body experience. It is not just a 'penis' experience. Women want to feel the pleasure of sexual climax of course, but few achieve orgasm through simple penile penetration and a few slamming jerks of the male hips. It needs more subtle style and care. Therefore by utilising new erotic techniques to please your partner and yourself,.. while worrying less about your erection,.. you can probably please her a lot more and that means you have become a better and more powerful lover.

Another plus of the Twenty-Minute Miracle Method is that it is completely natural. There are no dangerous drugs or chemicals, no injections, no gimmicks, no devices and no surgery. In other words, by deciding not to allow yourself to be defeated by a soft penis, you have actually been able to discover new heights in sexual pleasure

In this way, taking charge of your sex life can often be the solution not only to potency problems, but to problems such as decreased sex drive and sexual boredom.

Assuming control

Despite the more liberated approach that women have towards sex these days, they often appreciate a man who knows what he wants in bed. If you decide to have sex using the Twenty Minute Method, she'll probably be quite enthusiastic because she knows that you intend to seduce her, arouse her and please her. As an additional benefit, since the Method does not depend on a hard penis, you can now have sex whenever you want and as many times as you want. This is very useful in the case of a man whose partner is multi-orgasmic and wants several climaxes to his one. However, to keep the sex experience exciting and thrilling, it is strongly recommended that you read the following advice and suggestions carefully. Then comply with the advice. Finally, resolve to change your behaviour. In all seriousness, successfully resolving your potency problem in the long term may well depend upon it.

1. Have sex only when you feel aroused. Don't give it a half-hearted try just because you think you should do your duty. Disinterested sex can take the life right out of your penis. (Of course if your partner wants it badly it is only fair to compromise. Most partners who do,.. will usually get a kick out of co-operation and feeling used and appreciated,.. and what is more they often get very turned on when they experience their partner's urgent enthusiasm).
2. Have only the kinds of sex you want. Your partner must understand that it's essential for you to please yourself in order to resolve your potency problems. Moreover, it really is true that most women enjoy sex better when the man dictates what to do. This doesn't mean being domineering or dictatorial and is not permission to behave so selfishly. Gentle guidance is the correct measure. If something really turns you off or makes you nervous, don't do it,.. but think about it for a while. Analyse why it bothers you. Try to rationalise and overcome your doubts. They are really due to old ingrained fears and guilts,.. and are better replaced by logic and compromise.
3. Make sure that the sexual 'atmosphere' is right for you. If the general ambience of time, place, clothing, music, position, etc. have an effect on your own personal enjoyment, arrange them to suit you. Create your own personal and optimal sexual conditions.
4. Learn to recognise when you are tense. Learn how to relax yourself in tense situations. For example, if you get uptight when your partner plays with your penis, don't let her do it until you've learned to relax and come to like this activity. (Consider using auto-suggestion and hypnosis as in Chapter Six.)
5. Get the kind of stimulation you like and focus on it. Enjoying the best

will bring out the best in your penis. If you like 'dirty talk', a certain position, or technique, concentrate on getting that kind of stimulation. Then, while its happening to you, relax and focus on how good it feels.

In other words, you need to be able to take charge of sexual situations so that you are enjoying the experience as well as pleasing your partner.

Partners please note: his leadership will do you both good. Go along with it. This is no time for a spate of counterproductive female chauvinism. That is for those who need it; not for real people and certainly not for mature people.

* * *

This form of total re-training has immense benefits and many of them spill over into other aspects of life. An established but possibly threatened relationship is rejuvenated. The woman has been deeply involved in helping. The man feels honoured and grateful. Love and affection have a helpful environment in which to flourish and develop further. The relaxation periods calm fears, ease stresses and reduce daily anxieties and agitations. Improved sexual performance generates confidence. A man feels less need to make up for his sexual shortcomings by displays of aggression, grumpy frustration or even physical assertions of a violent or threatening mature. He is more of a man,.. and a better one at that.

Patiently based on a foundation of sound re-training over a period of weeks, these techniques virtually guarantee that any man with a penis and a partner can take the first step on the road back to sexual happiness,.. vaginal entry and good sex, in just twenty short minutes.

That is what we promised.That is what we delivered.

There is no better method anywhere.

* * *

Chapter Five

A WORD TO HER

Your man is in trouble!

He is in just as much trouble, maybe even more, as if he were going broke, going in for major surgery,.. or going to jail. You may not realise it yet but being impotent means he is in very big trouble indeed.

The most powerful of all your man's inborn, natural motivations is now being frustrated. He can't have sex. Things might even be so bad that that doesn't mean all that much to you. Well, it should. Because unless the situation is corrected, one way and another, it will cost you, your children, your home and your entire relationship and way of life a great deal. You will miss a vast treasurehouse of pleasure and happiness, physical and emotional. And in place of it you will find an unnecessarily heavy load of trouble, miseries, rows and doubts,.. all of them things that you could do without and which could be avoided.

Now, you are not listening to the prejudiced ramblings of a male chauvinist out to make women feel bad and to help men to more sex. Far from it. The writer of these pages is a man still happily married to the woman he has loved for thirty five years, the same family man who meets with his children most days of the week and who holidays with them and his grandchildren whenever they can all get leave at the same time. Furthermore, these words have been checked over by his wife to make sure he does not overstate, or accidentally mislead,.. or brag!

Some might think that a happy family, marriage and sex life are qualification enough to write on the subject. But there is more. For the writer is a qualified physician of over thirty years experience in medical practice. He has specialised in Sexual Medicine and worked in it most of his professional life. First, for several years, as an important part of his work as a family doctor in an English country town and later as a Senior Consultant with his own therapy clinic, and consulting rooms in the heart of London's prestigious Harley Street. He has been a contributor to countless magazines, books and periodicals, both medical and public. His work has appeared in everything from the British Medical Journal to Forum and from Penthouse and Vogue to the Journal of the Royal Society of Medicine. He has heard endless sad stories of ruined relationships, broken homes and human sadness. He has heard every kind of disaster explained by those who went through them. He has treated every kind of human problem.

It is from this vast compendium of experience that he feels able to write this book, and especially this section 'A Word to Her'. It is, in many ways, the most important part of the book. For success in overcoming impotence,.. as indeed for a happy sex-life to be established, relished and extended throughout life at all, depends almost entirely on the woman. It is you who holds the keys to happiness and success in this most fundamental need. The reverse is also true. Most of the therapies that I have seen fail have failed because of the absence of female effort and support.

Here then is the nub of the matter. Your man is in trouble. He almost certainly can't make it alone. He needs you. The reward for him will be restored sexual potency and an end to frustration. The reward for you will be far greater. Not only will he and your marriage and happiness be saved. You will have the added satisfaction of it all being your achievement. The fulfilment and happiness levels of your own life,.. and the security of your home, family and future will all have gone up immeasurably.

Oh yes, and there's one more thing. You will have learned a lot more about sex,.. and you will have come to enjoy it and reap its benefits more than you once thought possible. That is a promise.

Old methods... new style

So, what do you do? Three things that's all. The same three things you do almost instinctively and time after time in organising the needs of your own home,.. think, spring clean, re-furbish.

First things first,.. the thinking. By thinking, what is meant here is to assess the current situation and decide what you want out of it. Next comes an assessment of yourself. Finally comes your plan of future action. Let us assume since you are reading this book that the current situation is unsatisfactory. Your partner, for whatever reason, is impotent. You know it and you know all the hazards that impotence brings.

You want to stop all that and help things to be better. That's the situation assessed.

Now comes a harder bit, assessing yourself. Try completing the following questionnaire, just answering yes or no, right or wrong.

1. You are a decent, normal, respectable woman. Yes/No
2. You had some fairly serious love affairs in your years 15-20. Yes/No.
3. You came from a decent, normal, respectable, God-fearing home and family. Yes/No
4. Quite a number of your early affairs involved sex,.. whether just feeling each other or actually having intercourse. Yes/No.
5. Nowadays you don't mind sex now and again but its not that important. Right/Wrong.
6. You have a drawer full of black garter belts and flimsy underwear. Right/Wrong.
7. You had an ordinary, decent education. Yes/No.
8. You've several times gone topless on a topless beach. Yes/No
9. You believe in God and used to go to church or still do. Yes/No.
10. You often wear nothing around the house when your husband is home. Right/Wrong.
11. You believe that kinky sex is pretty perverted. Right/Wrong.
12. You and your husband often give each other oral sex. Right/Wrong.
13. You usually had a job before you were married. Yes/No.
14. You enjoy reading sexy books and seeing sexy pictures. Right/Wrong.
15. You are now a busy wife/mother. Yes/No
16. You often say swear words or dirty words. Right/Wrong.
17. You are your husband's wife,.. not his whore. Right/Wrong.
18. You have some rather strange sexual fantasies that you keep to yourself. Right/Wrong.
19. You regard doing deviant sex as something humiliating and degrading to women. Yes/No.
20. You like sex very much and often. Right/Wrong.

Scoring: For odd numbers (1,3,5, etc.) score 1 point for every 'Yes' or 'Right'.

For even numbers (2,4,6 etc.) score 1 point for every 'No' or 'Wrong'.

0-5 You are a great partner

6-10 With some changes you can be a great partner
11-15 With a determined effort you can be a great partner
16-20 Bad news. Radical re-think imperative.

A lot of things to learn

The point to be learned from that rough and ready test is that you may be a great wife and mother but you can still be a rotten sex partner. That is a dangerous pit-fall. Experience has shown literally thousands of women whose men left them although they were wonderful, family women,.. hard-working, reliable, thrifty,.. and often very beautiful. These things were just not enough. Time and again sex proved to be more vital than any of them.

There is another sad shock that has come to countless women. They thought their sex lives were OK, thank you. Untold numbers of women have experienced the bitterness of abandonment for another woman who was obviously just not their equal in any respect,.. except in bed. They are often utterly astonished. A book could be filled with quotes like "I never knew he cared much about sex" or "It always seemed enough to me and he never complained," or "I would have done this or that but he didn't ask and I never knew he wanted to."

Be certain, Ladies one and all, sex does matter to him. It matters immensely, profoundly,.. fundamentally. Man is a sexual animal,.. and woman too for that matter. He may not talk sexy, or look it or act it. He may say nothing. He may seldom make advances or suggestions. His sex habits may be brief, occasional and repetitively boring. But deep inside sex matters a great deal. He may even not be aware of it himself.

Be certain too that he has sexual fantasies of a kind that would make your eyes pop open. All men do,.. though many deny it. They fondly dream of things we shall soon discuss and which will amaze and probably disturb you. For men are very, very sexual. However little sex they get, it is still a powerful force in their lives. And for a sexual man to live in close relationship with a woman who is attractive to him is constantly to have his sexuality stirred and roused a dozen times a day. He sees you perfectly dressed, near, smelling female. He sees your breasts, your legs, your tempting zones. He wants you and he wants sex with you. Be convinced of it. Don't make the blunder of thinking things are 'alright' unless you are having lots of good, varied, intimate, wholesome sex. And don't dream for a moment that things are OK if he is impotent. That just can't be. Somewhere, and probably a very big somewhere, there is a need for your feminine wiles and abilities.

Why things are as they are

Soon we shall talk about things that are going to surprise you or maybe shock you speechless,.. perhaps they'll offend you too. But try to resist those automatic reactions. Try responding individually instead of like someone programmed to jump predictably when a certain string is pulled. When you are shocked, stop,.. at once, sharply,.. and think. Why are you shocked? Is it because things like whatever it is are supposed to shock you? Or because you were brought up to be silent and shy and ashamed of sex,.. which is a rather nasty stuff anyway?

If any of these or similar reasons are the explanations for being shocked they just won't do. Not anymore. You are you,.. an individual. You don't have to be shocked or disgusted just because someone said you are supposed to be. Nor because of the way you were programmed by the hypocrisy of society years and years ago. Now you are free,.. an independent, intelligent adult. You can think for yourself,.. consider new ideas,.. make your own decisions. And you certainly can't reject sexual things that affect your very life, marriage and family because of a lot of outdated, outmoded fashions,.. which were pretty hopeless even when they were new.

When you have thought about things you may feel very differently. At any rate it will have been your deliberate choice not an automatic knee-jerk response.

Make no mistake about it, sex has been around a long time and it looks like going on that way. It might be easier to join it since you can't beat it. There are good biological reasons for this. It is as though Old Mother Nature has recognised the value of the secure family unit based on a bonded pair of one man with one woman. She therefore made it easy for people to fall in love,.. by seeing each other, desiring each other and being thus attracted to each other. Stable relationships always start that way and progress from preliminary contacts to something greater. Then, having fallen in love, the biological aim is to stay in love. And Nature has designed no better way of re-enforcing a relationship than by sex. That is why humans don't have an occasional breeding season like most other animals, but are equipped to be ready and able to have sex anytime. It is the 'willing' bit that is sometimes left out.

So, it is in our genetic programme to give, receive and enjoy plenty of sex lots of the time for years and years. It is not some upshot modern idea due to over-sexedness. Not at all. It is truly Nature's way and to deny it is futile. Depriving someone, including oneself, of something as vital as sex does not make the desire go away. But instead of harnessing its great power for the good, denial twists it back, frustrated and dangerous, upon the people involved.

It is a sad thing to report, but about three-quarters of people literally never touch each other sexually except in bed. For them there are no cuddles or caresses, no warm and intimate stroking and fondling, often not so much as holding hands,.. and certainly no saucy touching of those awful 'private parts'.

Furthermore, people have dreadful difficulty in communicating about sex. A woman may dream of being held closely, seduced and thrilled by her husband who lusts after her,.. but she'd be far too shy to tell him. A man may fantasise day after day about coming home from work to find his wife naked, legs apart, on the bed. But he's far too afraid of scorn or rejection to tell her. Sex is something that from infancy we were misled into believing to be wrong, dirty and not a subject for discussion. We pay a huge collective fine for that imprinted nonsense.

Start the spring-cleaning

Those ideas you must abandon. Now you must get to the spring cleaning part of your re-organisation. And in that spring cleaning out must go all those old fashioned restraints, conditioned responses and children's rules that no longer apply. You must get back to being the wholesome, natural, sex-loving creature nature designed you to be. The Grundy-mentality and the Whitehouse style of 'Thou Shalt Not' have no place in the treatment of impotence.

Similarly the psychological jargon and the feminist misconception of recent years. Of course, woman has her rightful place, absolutely equal with men's. But to translate that fundamental equality into a load of strained and silly political theory is quite wrong. What is all this about it being in some way wrong to be a sex object,.. whatever that may be? It is part of everyone to be many different things. A woman will be, in any day, mother, cook, laundress, cleaner, shopper, secretary, car-washer, gardener. What is so wrong if she is a mistress and lover too? Why not be a sex object for a while now and then? Nature certainly has no objections. She made it that way. It is natural and good that way. It was misguided people who proclaimed it otherwise. If Nature is 'green' then sex is green too.

The things you prefer

Preferences are strange things. If you have a preference you can easily understand why. If you have no liking for a thing it is often rather hard to imagine what other people see in it. If you loath under-cooked liver the very thought of someone else eating it with relish amazes you. And what about eating octopus, frogs' legs, chocolate locusts,.. and a hare that has been fermented in its own blood until putrid? Some people like Chinese food, some don't.

Some people like certain sexual variations too. Others are indifferent and unmoved. The perpetual mediocrity of sameness doesn't bother them. A few are so revolted that they dismiss all variations as vile perversions,.. which is seldom the case. If you prefer intercourse flat on your back it probably seems pretty normal. But some regard it as disgusting to have a pillow beneath your hips in order to enjoy deeper penetration. And what of the woman who likes it best on her knees, or on top kneeling over her man? Is there anything wrong with that? Of course not. What then of the woman who likes the feel of a moist fingertip on her clitoris? Or of lips nibbling her nipples? What of the woman who likes to be undressed and 'taken' with a show of a bit of macho, masculine, he-man bravado. Is that bad? Or what if it excites her to have her bottom gently spanked,.. or to be blindfolded,.. or to do it in front of a mirror,.. or out in a field or a parked car? Can anyone say this woman is guilty of wrong-doing, wicked thinking,.. evil, sexual perversions? Certainly not. All are harmless ways to get the best out of a good thing.

After all, we spend time in the kitchen making up delicious dishes when all we really need are a few basic proteins and vitamins. We dress ourselves up in gorgeous fashions whereas all we really need is a blanket or a few animal skins.

Since we embellish and improve on all of nature's other gifts and needs why should sex be any different? No reason at all. Equally as logical as haute cuisine, or haute couture is 'haute-sex'.

Sexual preferences

This is all just as well as people do have very strong sexual preferences. These are often the subject of fantasies, those half-dreams, half-hopes, mostly imaginings of various sexual desires and escapades. Fantasies are wholesome things. In large part they remain as fantasies, the thrill being to think about them, to 'live' them in secret or at most to share them by talking about them. For a woman to have secret fantasies about being multiple-raped by a dozen Red Indian braves doesn't mean that given half a chance she'd be on the next plane to Arizona. For a man to fantasise about being serviced by three beautiful women at the same time doesn't mean he's saving up on the petrol money to buy himself the services of three such co-operative sex-merchants.

So whatever you do, don't be ashamed or secretive about your fantasies,.. or about his. Try to enjoy them, understand them,.. share them. And if you both find you can help the other to act out those fantasies in your own bedroom, then do it. Fun and games, variations and deviations, are the sauces and pickles of the sexual diet. They reward both partners. And as measures towards the relief of impotence, they are very, very successful.

When sex is really good it is entirely fair for a woman to indulge her sexual preferences. She should expect her partner to co-operate, compromise and see that her choices are satisfied just as certainly as his. When sex is not good because of his impotence, there is nothing for it but for her to find every way possible to encourage and satisfy his preferences. Later, when he is well, she can have her share again too. But for the time being, we are talking here of treating his impotence. So we shall be considering his preferences only. (That is due to space not to chauvinism!)

A few years ago, as part of a major data-collection programme, a large number of men from every walk of life,.. the sexy, the undersexed, the wealthy, the clever, the accountant, the soldier, were all 'screened' for their sexual habits, fantasies and preferences. It turned out that of all the enormous numbers and combinations of possible sexual variations, a mere half-dozen featured really strongly. They were common to most men whereas the more remote practices appealed to very few. It is these half-dozen techniques that it would be wise for women to know, recognise and understand. After that they will be at their disposal,.. weapons of tremendous power in the battle against impotence, and for a lasting and rewarding sex life.

Big surprises

Now you are about to be shocked,.. so be prepared.

By far the commonest male preference whether fantasy or for real is oral sex. Yes, you heard,.. that was 'oral sex'. It was the main preference of more than a huge 92% of all men of all ages. It means either you having him kiss, suck and lick your vagina which is called cunnilingus, or it means you have his penis in your mouth, which is called fellation. Like it or not, to bring the face, nose and mouth close to the genital organs of a partner is a deeply embedded animal impulse. Most higher animals have it,.. and we are the highest animals of all. We certainly have it.

Of course hygiene matters but that is easily taken care of. With that proviso, there is absolutely nothing wrong with oral sex. There is no more profoundly pleasurable a sensation for those who enjoy it,.. and most come to do so, than this extremely intimate form of love-making. Many people find they are aroused faster, and orgasm more deeply, either by these methods or with their help than any other.

Some women fear they may cause pain to those male organs they've been told are so sensitive. Fears are unfounded. Firm, gentle stroking and sucking of the penis shaft, head and testicles cause no discomfort. Some women too are fearful in case he might come in their mouths. As long as you have no objection there is nothing wrong with that. It is totally harmless and so is semen. Plenty of women find it both sexually satisfying and a source of some pride that they can both cause the ejaculation and receive it. Swallow if you like, it is absolutely safe, and respectable. Be sure he will adore you for what you do. And the sight of his face as he feels himself in your warm mouth or as he ejaculates onto your welcoming tongue or loving face will be an experience you too can come to treasure,.. as many women already do.

The second male preference, scoring eighty five per cent of all men, is for some form of voyeurism,.. the male response to female sexual display. In the animal world the female is seldom beautiful or given to sexual showing off. It is the males that do that. Humans are different. Both sexes do it. It is in fact the first method of biological contact in humans. Each sees the other and is attracted by certain features. It is fashionable nowadays to say it's a woman's sense of humour or her personality that first attract; or for a woman to proclaim she was attracted by his courtesy and good manners. Doubtless these do matter. But at a deeper level she was attracted, even if she didn't know it or denies it, by his angular shape, height, build, his beard perhaps, the sight and odour of his body, and so on. He was attracted by her smooth curves, her bottom, breasts and legs and by her sense of available vulnerability.

It is a shrewd woman who makes use of this power she has to attract visually and sexually. She should take every opportunity to display herself. His obvious excitement will excite her. It is easy to know how and what does it. Buy a couple of men's glossy magazines. They are full of what women see as repetitive pictures emphasising the same parts of the body and by models in the same sorts of clothes. The reason those photographs are so similar is because they are what almost all men like. Your man will probably have preferences amongst them but he'll go for most of them to some extent or other. Try a few out on him.

The great favourites are high-heel shoes or boots, stockings, and garter-belts. Mini-skirts rate very high,.. and it is utter nonsense to imagine that you won't look sexy in one if your legs are a bit plump or skinny. A man reacts with very different assessments than the shape-or fashion-conscious woman. He'll like you in a mini, you can be sure. Scanty panties, peep-hole bras, fishnet undies, neck chokers, wet T-shirts,.. are all other high-score possibilities. So are fur, leather or latex clothes, studded belts and anklets. And remember, though the clothes may excite him, arouse him and make him better,.. it's the you inside them he's really after.

Let him see you. Be naked or lightly clad. Let him watch you dress, undress, bath,.. urinate. Sit with your legs showing,.. stocking-tops and all. Lie on the bed with your legs open. Encourage him to look. Show him a glossy magazine and say "I've always wanted to be a model,.. could you photograph me to look like that,.. I'd love you to try." Then stand back and see how fast he finds a camera.

Throw away your old, everyday underwear. Try tying a wide black ribbon around your waist and pulled up tight between your thighs. Wear just your high heels when you take him his afternoon coffee. Cut an old pair of shorts waist to waist back to front so things peep out provocatively. Cut breast holes in a T-shirt. Buy some ropes or netting or chains and wrap them around yourself. Try shaving off your pubic hair too, not just that in your armpits.

Use the gifts Mother Nature gave you. Be sure you will get more response from showing him your vagina than from a hundred repetitions of 'I love you darling'. He will vastly prefer the sight of your sexily clad and welcoming body than a second helping of your best egg and tuna salad.

Shocking habits?

Next in order of men's sexual preferences is, to some, the most shocking of all,.. anal sex. It is an example of a well-known but unexplained natural phenomenon. The outside of the body is covered with dry skin. The inside is lined with moist 'skin' called mucous membrane. Where these meet, at the body orifices, are the areas which are both erogenous to the owner, that is which yield pleasurable sensations, and are also target areas for the partner's sexual advances. Eskimos rub noses. Primitives in Borneo and Sarawak greet each other with what looks like a kiss-on-both-cheeks in best French tradition,.. though they are really touching ears. Kissing is best known of all these unexplained contacts. Penis, vagina and urethral openings too are all erotic zones. And so, quite definitely, is the one remaining orifice, the anus.

The objections to anal sex come from several sources. To start with, in some countries it is an illegal act punishable by imprisonment. Nothing in this book should be regarded as in any way advising any reader to break laws however stupid they are. In England for example, it is in order for one man to insert his penis into another man's backside as long as the act is done with mutual consent and in private. However, if that same man's wife asks him to put his penis in her anus, he could go to jail for it. No wonder ordinary folk get confused.

Another objection is that it is not 'natural'. This too is hard to understand. The desire is very natural indeed. Millions of men have it. And millions of women love it too. The act is very similar to vaginal intercourse which is also very natural. Objection on the grounds that it is a homosexual tendency are nonsense. The man who loves anal sex with his wife is invariably revolted by the idea of having it with another man. Furthermore, homosexual men don't want anything to do with female parts, anus or anywhere else. Apart from a very few AC/DC individuals the distinction is very precise and absolute.

Finally there is the objection that it is unhygienic. This is certainly arguable. But then so is most sex. It is a medical fact that there are astonishingly few pathological bacteria, that is dangerous germs, in any of the body openings. There are so many more in the mouth and nose than anywhere else that, during kissing, doctors shudder to think of the bacteria count! The vagina too harbours infectious organisms much of the time. So can the smegma, the white, cheesy substance that collects under the foreskin of the penis and clitoris. The anus usually has fewer than all of these others. Additionally, the anus itself, especially when washed regularly, seldom contains any faecal material. That is usually much higher up and out of the way.

Other than for the nonsensical legal position then, there are no valid objections whatsoever to anal sex. Most couples who are experienced in sexual activity enjoy it at least occasionally, more often regularly. And so they can, for enjoyable it most certainly is. Like vaginal intercourse it may start out being a little strange or uncomfortable for the uninitiated woman. It is beyond the scope of this book to explain the suitable training methods and these can be found well described in other books, for example 'Age and Sex' by Dr. Richard Silurian. (See Sources List).

It is, however, very much within the scope of this book to tell how enjoyable anal sex is, how much it is desired,.. and how very effective it is in the struggle against impotence.

Remember yet again, he will probably be far too shy and afraid of humiliating refusal, to ask you. As usual, the first moves will probably be up to you. Here are some tips. Find a novel in which anal sex is mentioned and some heroine enjoying it. Then ask his advice "Do people really do that?'' or ''I wonder if I'd like that, would you?'' or ''Would you help me try it sometime?'' Another way is, when his fingers are fondling your vagina, you can take his hand and rub one finger around your anus or into it. Squirm appreciatively and say it felt good. Alternatively, actually during intercourse you can slip his penis out of you with one hand, press its head against your anus and bear down on it. It may not go in without plenty of lubrication but the chances are that he'll get the message very quickly.

No more 'self-abuse'

The next preference listed by men, and again, a very widespread one, is masturbation done either personally or by his partner and to himself or to his partner. There is, quite simply, not a single bad thing to be said against masturbation. It is an entirely good, natural and wholesome activity and one that is to be thoroughly recommended. Where partners take widely different times to be aroused, the slower partner can masturbate beforehand to hasten matters. If one is insufficiently satiated when the encounter is over, masturbation can add a beneficial little extra. When one partner needs to orgasm, twice a day, the other twice a week it eases the balance. It does the same when one or other partner is temporarily unavailable for sex, say due to work or illness. It is good practice. It is good fun.

And it has one other immense advantage. Mutual masturbation,.. simultaneous masturbation of each partner by the other, is an essential part of most love-making occasions. It is the way to explore, arouse, excite and sometimes even satisfy. A man will get a great thrill from making his woman come as his fingers stimulate her vagina. Many women will be immensely rewarded and will orgasm themselves just by watching their man ejaculate into their caressing hands. It is an act of considerable beauty and power.

A great deal can also be learned from watching a partner masturbate. No-one knows better which bits feel best and how. Ask to watch how he does it. Ask him to watch you. Show, tell, explain, and things will get better yet. And as for impotence therapy,.. it's wonderful. For example, when you are out somewhere, in the car perhaps, in the cinema, in a park, it is probably impossible to have intercourse, so he will not be under any pressure or expectation to perform. Now, slip your hand into his trousers pocket and fondle him. The response may surprise you, and he'll be very pleased at the new adventurous you. One more nail driven into the coffin of his impotence.

Talking dirty

Swear words, rude words, offensive expressions and the like are somehow exciting. We were brought up not to use them, though most of us do from time to time. The point is that when we do they give this sense of thrill, of freedom, of rejection of authority. Whatever the deep explanations for this, rude words have a great deal of appeal. Nowhere is this more true than sex. Just think how many rude words are sexual,.. cock, dick, cunt, fuck,.. and so on. Nice girls don't say such things. True,.. maybe. But sexy girls do. And that is the point.

Using doubtful language, so-called 'talking dirty', is the next commonest male preference. It is also, like oral sex and anal sex, high on the preference list of experienced women. So this is a practice that promises added pleasure for both. And it doesn't stop there. Reading sexy poetry, or an erotic book or seeing pornographic movies or magazines can add to the pleasure several times over.

Don't keep silent about sex. Talk about it. Tell him things. Tell him what you like, don't like, fantasise about, would like to try. And, at least from time to time, do it in down-to-earth language. Its an odd thing but lots of people will say 'Fuck' when they touch something hot or the milk boils over. They will use fuck-words as a verb, a noun, an adjective, a participle,.. but never, absolutely never, to describe what it is, sexual intercourse. People are strange. Nevertheless talking dirty is powerfully erotic and is a distinct turn on for many couples. Try it. Ask him things. Make 'dirty' promises.. 'I want to suck you off and swallow your spunk' or 'I want your cock up me' or 'I need to feel your tongue in my cunt', or 'When you come home tonight I want you to fuck me silly, up my arse,.. in front of the mirror'. It may be hard to start with but it gets easier the more you do it. And it really doesn't hurt at all.

A taste for cruelty?

Sado-masochism (SM) or sexual cruelty can be taken to the most savage and vicious extremes. bsolutely nothing in this book should be construed as condoning or recommending any form of sexual practice which involves bodily injury or serious pain. Such things are all very well as fantasies and they are very common as such. Put into practice they are the unacceptable manifestations of a person out of control and perhaps dangerous.

That being clearly understood, SM can play a big role in human sexual relations. Some aspect of sexual SM is the next choice on the male preference list. No-one has ever worked out exactly how, but there is a definite connection between sex and violence. It is probably very ancient and genetically imprinted into the background of even such higher creatures as ourselves. Just watch a horse and mare, mating dogs or 'treading' doves and you will see the snapping, biting, clawing, grasping and feather-ripping that goes on. These mirror those grunting, shrieking, biting, tugging and convulsing actions that accompany human intercourse.

These feelings, whatever their explanation, are certainly there. They are natural and they are in us all. So why not adapt them for use. Gentle pain, simulated force, bondage and submission games all have their place in the varied armamentarium of the sexually adventurous couple. And they very much have their place in the treatment of impotence.

Everyone knows the simplest of SM manifestations,.. slave bracelets,.. and that is what they are. The SM association accounts for their universal popularity. Make sure you have several. Ankle chains,.. also emulated by ankle straps on high heel shoes, are another good idea. So is a chain belt worn around a bare midriff. Fishnet stockings emphasise the netted or captured look. Why not see if he would like to be blindfolded and tied to the bed while you masturbate him. Why not ask him to tie you down on the floor, widely spread-eagled and exposed or with your wrists tied behind your back, and let him use his electric shaver on your pubic hair. Try dressing up in a harem outfit or a 'french maid' black mini and white apron. You might even try spanking his bottom or asking him to spank yours. Try tying ropes or light chains around your waist and thighs and breasts. Wear a few leather straps. And just watch the effect on him,.. and on yourself.

Sexual aids

There is another series of sexual tricks that can be added to the female, and indeed the joint, repertoire. This is as good a spot as anywhere to draw them to her attention and explain them.

Sexual Aids are devices designed to improve performance in and enjoyment of sexual activities. Some are meant for men, others for women, while clearly some affect both. To start with here are particularly mentioned vibrators and dildos, the most favoured female aids,.. and those which are next on the male preference list.

A vibrator is a phallic-shaped toy, an imitation penis. There are small ones, perhaps three inches long for clitoral or anal use. There are massive ones, some ten or twelve inches long and nearly three inches in diameter. But those most preferred for most circumstances are of average penis size,.. say six or seven inches long and up to an inch and a half in diameter. The tapering shaft is usually smooth and at one end is a switch. When in the 'on' position, the contained battery powers a tiny, buzzing electric motor with an off-centred weight. The revolving weight makes the whole shaft vibrate. The frequency of vibration is important. Less than forty cycles tends to produce little effect. Around fifty to sixty cycles most women find the sensation against the vaginal lips and clitoris or well up inside the vagina to be sexually exciting. In spite of popular opinion and the availability of variable speed vibrators, increasing the cyclic rate much above sixty cycles does not further increase excitement.

A dildo is an actual imitation penis. They too come in an enormous variety of sizes, rigidity, colours and textures. Some are very pliable and are almost life-like in feel. Others are rigid and unyielding. There are flesh-coloured ones, black ones and even some that illuminate in the dark. There is a particularly valued dildo which is curved and designed to angle forward and stimulate the elusive G-spot in those who seek it or are already aware that they have the necessary area and are able to locate it.

Once the instinctive shame and shyness are overcome and once women become accustomed to using one or more vibrators or dildos, almost all will find they can masturbate and orgasm with them very successfully indeed. To give occasional displays of this type can have an effect on the watching partner out of all proportion to the effort involved. All advanced sex women should have some such items, should use them, and should show off in using them. All advanced sex men expect it,.. and should. They must, of course, also be prepared to play all aspects of the masturbation game themselves.

There is another use of aids, particularly for men. If his problem is that the penis is physically too small the only real solution is to undertake a radical penis enlarging and training programme,.. Penatone for example, such as is dealt with more extensively elsewhere in this book. But for those unable to undergo training the smaller penis can have its length or its girth, or both, increased by wearing a sexual aid known as an extension sheath. This consists of a firm, rubber condom-like sheath the sides or tip of which are extended to the required dimensions. Similarly there is available a hollow dildo into which the flaccid or totally impotent penis is inserted. When held in position by a light belt a simulated or assisted penetration is certainly possible.

It is often repeated failure to erect and penetrate that amplifies and prolongs sexual problems. By using one of these aids actually to introduce a partially erected or even totally soft penis into the vagina, perhaps for the first time in years, it is frequently possible to break the vicious circle, renew hope, improve sensation and generate a new and therapeutic confidence in success.

There is a considerable further range of sexual aids. Some of these are of definitely practical value others are principally for fun,.. some are both. Padded extension sheaths worn by men yield greater bulk on penetration for the smaller man or the more capacious woman. There are also a variety of rings for wearing by the man and which are designed to give extra sensation to the female partner. Some are worn around the sulcus or groove behind the penis head, others are fitted around the base of the penis. The former actually stroke the inside of the vagina during coital movements; the latter have padded or profiled areas to stimulate the labia and clitoral regions when pressed against them during deep penetration.

Some ideas are highly erotic in appearance, as for example, the Arab Strap. This is a cradle of formidable-looking black leather straps and studs which enmeshes the penis and affords it a caged and restrained yet exaggeratedly aggressive appearance. There is also a long narrow shaft with a wrinkled surface that can be attached by a harness so that it protrudes like an extra, thinner penis suspended below the real one. This enables both the vagina and the anus to be penetrated and stimulated at the same time,.. which is a sensation much appreciated by the many who grow to like it.

The entire list of sexual aids is long and varied. Don't be fooled by the old drivel that they just are not natural. Of course they are not. But then neither is pruning apple trees, wearing glasses or driving a motor-car. They're still pretty useful things though, aren't they? And crutches are unnatural too,.. yet which handicapped person would dream of being without them? See sexual aids in the same way.There is something there for everyone and it is largely a matter of selection and trying the ideas that most appeal. Certainly no advanced sex couple intent upon eliminating the impotence of the male partner would be without a selection that can further extend their sexual repertoire.

The final formula

To conclude, the overall secret for women in sex is spoken of as all the double-u's. Be warm, willing, welcoming and wanton. Don't hesitate to cuddle him in the night and cradle his penis in your hand. If he is near you, day or night, take his hand and put it on your breast, or snuggle it between your legs, even making sure one fingertip finds its way inside the front door. When he's watching TV sit and stroke his trousers, or open them, take out his penis and suck it. Or suck him before he wakes in the morning. An erection may well be the result. Try wandering around the house in nothing but your panties and high heels. Sleep naked.

Never make the mistake of thinking these sexy overtures are indecent. They are your innate sexuality, surfacing perhaps after years of suppression. The fancy clothes, and chains and sex toys are the catalysts to his renewed potency and to your enjoyment of each other.

And turn your back on the idea that being a little whorish for him is unfeminine. He will adore the whore in you,.. and there is a little in every woman. There is nothing humiliating or degrading in showing your body, using all its orifices, behaving sexily. Is it right or wrong to satisfy the very sexual urges that can help your partner back to normality? Of course it is right. Games of temporary humiliation and pretences at submission and degradation are nothing more than that,.. games. The real humiliation is for you to turn your back on his trouble and to withhold your vital help. The real humiliation is when he neglects or ignores or insults you in public or in private. Play-acting is totally different,.. and no act is too degrading to do for a loved partner.

Of course, nothing written here obliges you, the female reader, to do anything. Some will still say "I'm not wearing sexy knickers for anybody" or "Nobody is going to put his dick in my mouth" or "He can keep his fingers away from my bum, and that's that."

This book can't tell you what to do, but it can explain the options and offer ideas.

This book can't tell you what to think,.. but it can tell you what to think about.

The rest is up to you.

* * *

Chapter Six

THE MAGICAL EXTRAS

In the treatment of impotence, and indeed generally for anyone interested in maintaining a high degree of health and sexual vigour, there are certain additional ideas, techniques and therapies available. Few know about these. They are the tricks used by doctors on themselves and their own families,.. though by no means all doctors know much about them or even believe in them, so well kept secrets have some of them proved. Until recent years the only way to get such therapies was by visiting extremely expensive private clinics in Switzerland or the Bahamas. They are seldom if ever advertised to the public. They are the realm of experts and people who are 'in the know'. Some are costly; many are nowadays within the reach of almost everyone. They are the knacks and methods used by the upper echelons of society,.. the wealthy, the show business folk, top executives and senior operatives in every walk of life.

Here we call them 'The Magical Extras' for that is what they are. Anyone can manage without them. But if you use them you really will find these extras to be most advantageous,.. virtually magical sometimes in the benefits they confer. Try some and see.

REGENERATIVE THERAPY

The best of all is a form of treatment called Regenerative Therapy or RT for short. This is widely used by top people everywhere. Some large companies, well aware of the beneficial effects on their senior staff, offer them courses of RT at company expense. Some even treat the wives too! Everyone over the age of fifty (and younger still is better), should have a course of RT once a year at least. It is well worth the time and cost.

RT consists of a series of injections (suppositories are also available as an alternative), usually four on any treatment day, and given once a week over a period of four weeks. There is a good deal of flexibility in timing. For the most part the injections are virtually painless and have no unpleasant side-effects. They contain extracts and anti-sera of body cells in concentrated form. The cell extracts are manufactured in Germany under their most stringent pharmaceutical regulations and by the method developed by Professor Dyckerhof of Cologne University. As cells grow, they too become old and less efficient. New cells are created whenever needed by the process of replication,.. the existing, older cells literally dividing into two to make two new ones. The cells replicate themselves exactly,.. skin cells forming new skin cells, liver cells forming liver cells, and so on. The copying process depends on vital molecules in the cell nuclei called RNA (ribonucleic acid) and DNA. But tiny mistakes do get made. Some of these errors escape correction and, in turn, are copied. Gradually they accumulate from cell generation to generation just as if they were perfect. There is thus a general ageing and decline in cell integrity. RNA can now be extracted from healthy young cells and injected back into the muscles thereby permitting a far more accurate degree of replication to be resumed.

The effects of RT are often astonishing. Some people feel benefit within days though most undergo gradual changes after about six to eight weeks and as new cells 'come on line'. Benefits reported include higher exercise tolerance, better memory and concentration, substantially enhanced sexual performance, better appetite, improved sleep patterns, better skin texture and complexion, increased efficiency at work and a general, all-round improvement in sheer zest for and quality of life. Some say that RT actually extends the life span and this seems likely to be confirmed as research proceeds.

However, whether or not it puts more years in your life, it is already certain that it puts more life in your years! For those few who feel no benefit there is no form of dependency and therefore no need to repeat the courses. There is another hidden advantage. Using, as it does, the body immune system, RT acts, in a way, rather like having a vaccination. When someone has injections against say, tetanus, at the end of a month or two they don't feel any different. No benefit is felt. But the fact remains that they are different. They have benefited. They are now resistant to tetanus. The same happens in RT. Even the very few who don't feel any benefit are, in fact, different. Their tissues have been made more responsive, more functional, more efficient and more resistant to the wear and tear of existence. No-one is without these advantages although some may be advantages that cannot be actually felt. Over a long period however RT users are well convinced of the very real benefits. The cost of a treatments varies from as little as about three hundred and fifty pounds (six hundred dollars) for younger and healthy people to over five hundred (eight hundred and fifty dollars) for those who are older or less fit to start with.

For those who have no geographical access to injection courses treatments can also be given by the rectal suppository route. Although these are somewhat less effective than the injections they are a viable and excellent alternative and should not be missed by those living overseas and who cannot therefore attend in person.

WARNING: There are self-styled clinics in London and elsewhere offering these and similar courses at extortionate prices. Some are headed by medically non-qualified quacks and con-men who do not hesitate to exploit the old, the sick and the frightened with worthless substitute programmes for huge fees. Some even employ qualified doctors and pay them handsomely to act as 'respectable' front-men. It is a deplorable practice and should be forbidden by law. When you go for RT be certain you are treated by a properly qualified physician and, if you are charged more than five hundred pounds, suspect that you are being cheated. (See Sources List).

For the sexually conscious there are two specialised forms of RT that can be used to concentrate particularly on the sexual system tissues. As they too are in suppository form and of narrower, specific target zones, they are far less costly than ordinary, full therapeutic courses. Costs are also kept down as demand ensures that they can be manufactured in far larger and more economical quantities. There are several varieties available, the best being known as Masculone and Feminone, as their names suggest, designed for men and for women respectively. These suppositories are of high quality, being manufactured in Switzerland under the well-known, scrupulously precise supervision of the pharmaceutical department of the Swiss Government Health Authority.

Masculone contains tissue-specific antisera from the entire range of male sexual tissues,.. testicle, erectile tissue, nerve supply tissue, spinal cord and so on. Feminone is similar but of course contains ovary tissue in place of testicular. A full course is about thirty suppositories, one every second or third night. The failure rate,.. and every medical treatment does have a failure rate,.. is very low, almost everyone feeling at least some degree of benefit. This is usually noticed starting within the first two weeks. However these preparations are only designed and expected to work on those whose sexuality is below par. Nothing will raise the sexual level of output and performance above what is the proper maximum in their given circumstances. It is fair to say, in view of this, that virtually everyone will benefit who needs to. Conversely, those who do not benefit, do not because they are already at peak. At worst then these suppositories afford an excellent test of sexuality.

They either do you a lot of good, or, if they don't appear to help they have at least shown you that you are pretty good anyway. For this reason the present writer suggests a first investment in only ten suppositories and the rest of the course to follow providing that the new user is amongst the successful ones. (See Sources List).

THE ENERGISING RING

In Chapter Five there were mentioned at some length sexual aids and their value in an advanced sexual repertoire such as is best adopted in the attack on impotence. Pride of place amongst male aids unquestionably goes to the Energising Ring (or Blakoe Ring). The ring was first devised by a Dr. Blakoe working in Europe during the 1930s. Because of the taboo on sexual matters it was known to very few. Advertising was prohibited although the beneficial effect of the ring on impotence cases was and is often astounding. Men went on suffering as they just did not know help even existed. It was not until the 1960s that men learned about the ring. Since then thousands upon thousands have been worn with a very high success rate.

Originally the ring consisted a stout ebonite surround shaped to fit snugly around the root of the penis and scrotum together. A series of small, thermo-coupled metal plates embedded in the ring respond to body warmth and produce tiny but detectable galvanic currents. These currents are too small to be felt, but they are measurable with the correct instruments. They are generated throughout the time the ring is worn. Modern materials and manufacturing have much improved the ring which now comes in an adjustable form and with a open-and-close fastening. New and improved designs appear every few years as technology produces better methods and greater knowledge. The electro-magnetic effect has also been substantially enhanced and seeks to improve circulation to the male hormone (testosterone) producing tissues. The effect of the ring mechanically too in assisting, maintaining and pro-longing erection could be advantageously tried by every man after middle age,.. and for impotence sufferers at any age. There is a further advantage in that many women regard the ring as a powerfully erotic adornment and admire the way it holds the turgid penis erect and aggressively forward as well as encouraging greater inflation and there-fore size and staying power. The response can be quite dramatic. Indeed, it is probably the first treatment of choice in impotence, before any other more complex techniques are even considered. (See Sources List).

PENIS ENLARGEMENT AND TRAINING

Frequently there is more to a man's problem than his inadequate erection. One of the causes of recurrent or long-term impotence is concern over penis size. Sometimes too there is a need for training or re-training the penis. The Energising Ring helps but is not designed to achieve these two aims. In the opinion of the present writer, another method has the best success rate he has so far encountered. This method, known as the Penatone Programme (See Sources List) is not merely an erection method, though it is certainly that too, but is a full penis training programme. Two kinds of men benefit from using it,.. those who suffer from impotence and some other sexual problems,.. and those men of all ages who simply want to train the penis to be the biggest and best it can possibly be.

Penatone aims at aiding erection with an extremely effective vacuum device and at the same time using techniques aimed at penis enlargement and improvement. During the training there is a marked increase in blood flow to the penis with consequent increase in the penis' blood-space tissues and their capacity. This in turn means extra size. Muscles increase both in size and in power and greater control of them is learned. Sensation is developed as part of the same programme. Much can be achieved over a few weeks, the muscles trained and toned up, the sensitivity increased and the staying power in terms of duration of erection considerably lengthened.

It is an interesting fact that all over the world men are always seeking ways to enlarge the penis. If big is beautiful, bigger still is even better! Logical and theoretical arguments often revolve around the advantages of a big penis. Some say it matters, others that it is not at all important. Three major points emerge from all the chat. First that a the penis can be enlarged, trained and improved in performance. Second and most significant of all, irrespective of facts, whatever they be, men consider penis size to be important,.. therefore it is. That makes it so. Finally, men traditionally regard themselves as small, wish to be bigger and consequently seek methods of enlargement.

One argument often used to belittle this perpetual male desire for the big penis is that penis size does not matter to women. This is clearly not true. Just look at the personal ads in my contact magazine. A very high proportion of female advertisers specify that they seek only men who are well-endowed. It is true that women of limited experience maybe after contact with only one or two male organs throughout their entire lives, never have the chance to learn that there is any difference. But to those who are experienced, size matters a great deal. Other things, women tend to agree matter a great deal too,.. technique, respect, affection. But other things being equal, those with the experience to tell say 'better a good big one than a good small one'.

As every man wants to appear good in bed and as none will enjoy being unfavourably compared with previous sex partners, it is sure that men will always go on seeking ways to enlarge and improve the penis. The subject has been most entertainingly and comprehensively dealt with the the excellent book 'The Penis' by Dr. Dick Richards (See Sources List.) which is to be highly recommended. Similarly recommended is the Penatone Programme and its advanced continuation programme, Maxitone. Already, above, has been described the 'Energising Ring' and its erection creating and maintaining abilities. It is mentioned here again as its value in conjunction with the Penatone Programme has proved so considerable,.. as too has Masculone, also explained above. The combination of Penatone with Masculone and an Energising Ring probably cannot be bettered as a first try for men who seek to be at their sexual best.

FEMALE PROBLEMS

There is also a common female problem which might well need attention and which, in affected couples, can be most successfully treated at the same time. This is the matter of the 'weak pelvic floor' and its consequences. If you were able to look at a human skeleton you would notice that the pelvis is in fact a kind of bowl made of bones. But the bowl has no bottom! Anything you put in it would fall straight through. In the living body the bottom of the bowl consists of several complex sheets of muscle, tough, and elastic in consistency, which stretch across the 'missing' areas and seal them. In the female these sheets of muscle are perforated by the three body openings, the urethra to void urine, the rectum to void faeces and the vagina for sexual-reproductive purposes.

As a woman ages, or if she becomes overweight, if she suffers from constipation, and if she has gone through the pressures of childbirth once or twice, it is very likely that the straining involved will have weakened the muscle sheets. When they lose elasticity there arises the condition known as pelvic floor sag. The uterus, the bladder and sometimes the rectum too droop down lower in the pelvis to the extent that the cervix of the womb may even appear at the vaginal orifice.

This has a number of considerable inconveniences. Sudden physical efforts, running upstairs, coughing and sneezing cause the leakage of small quantities of urine. Tennis is out of the question. The constant soiling of clothing and the associated odours make social contacts very embarrassing. Sexually the vagina loses its grip and the slack orifice correspondingly affords only reduced sensation levels to its owner. The partner too quickly misses the delight of pressure on his entering penis. If the uterus has sagged down he cannot enter anyway as the vaginal space is already filled by the displaced uterus. The overall decrease in sexual pleasure comes at a time in life when such limitations are notably counter-productive. Statistics suggest at least one woman in six suffers at some stage of life or other,.. mostly in silence as only one in ten of those goes to her doctor about it.

There are a number of methods of treating pelvic floor sag. The commonest is the insertion of a ring or pessary. This is pushed up the vagina then braced fore and aft against the spine at the back and the pubic bones in front, thereby propping up the drooping organs. It is a generally successful method. But it does mean frequent removals for cleaning and to adjust size as time goes by. As with any foreign body there is a tendency to infection in the vagina and commonly an unpleasant smelling discharge of pus and vaginal debris troubles the patient and those of her associates within smelling range. Under these conditions, sex appears to become less desirable

Surgical repair or colporrhaphy is the ultimate medical solution. In this the sagging muscles are exposed and dissected out, drawn together firmly and stitched into their new positions. Although not a dangerous operation the discomfort of surgery in this tender zone can be well imagined. Nevertheless results are generally good.

Before resorting to either pessaries or surgery, there is now a far superior first line of defence. The cause of the problem is weak muscles. Of all parts of the body muscles are amongst the easiest and most successful to train so why not re-train the muscles to do their own job properly again? This is the sound argument that has resulted in the development of such concepts as Kegel exercises, Faradism and the new Gynatone methods of therapy. Re-training has proved to be successful in up to 40% of cases. It saves surgery, sex lives and happy marriages.

Decades ago Kegel introduced his exercise programme for the pelvic muscles. His method was simple but moderately effective. However being proposed at a time when discussion of sexual matters was frowned upon and most ladies ignored rather than sought treatment for 'trouble down below' the idea never caught on. Faradism has had similar, undeserved lack of wide acceptance. It involves electrical muscle stimulation through the perineal area, the resulting contractions being intended to re-train the weak tissues.

In recent years a new concept has been developed. The same group of doctors who developed Penatone and other devices, got together to devise a home treatment for pelvic floor sag. They collected every known idea then tested them rigorously. Many were discarded, some adopted, some adapted. Eventually the useful methods that had passed all the tests were assembled into an overall programme that was inexpensive and could be used by the woman in the privacy of her own home and without visits to doctors or the need for outside help. This is the Gynatone Programme, which has since had the approval not only of doctors and gynaecologists but of many, many users world wide. It has also been extensively acclaimed in medical journals. It should certainly be used by sufferers before they opt for other more heroic and costly methods. An alternative to the use of Gynatone is training with a series of insertable vaginal weight cones. Suppliers will be found in the Sources List.

APHRODISIACS

Aphrodisiacs are declared by some to be non-existent. They are fondly believed to exist by many others. The fact is that aphrodisiacs do exist in that there are things which improve human sexual arousal, response, staying power, performance and pleasure. Detailed discussion is beyond the scope of this book and is far better covered elsewhere (See Bibliography List).

The unfortunate thing is that many aphrodisiacs and substances have side-effects that are dangerous in doses that are likely to have any effect. Spanish Fly (cantharides) is so dangerous that there are liable to be criminal charges of murder in the event of mishap. Gold and silver salts, so popular with Asiatic populations, can cause heavy metal poisoning if only from the toxic contaminants like lead and tin that they frequently contain. Ginseng can cause insomnia, diarrhoea and blood pressure. Alcohol works in small doses as probably do Pethidine and Strychnine though poisoning by these is too likely to justify the risk.

Some foods are known to have aphrodisiac qualities and so have some herbal decoctions. A new technique is currently being developed and holds out perhaps the greatest possible hope. A panel of doctors, pharmacists, herbalists and homoeopaths recently pooled their knowledge and experience. After scouring the extensive literature they selected the most successful known ingredients. These herbal remedies have been subjected to extraction and potentisation radionically and are now under test as homoeopathic drops taken under the tongue or in small tablets.

It is expected that they will combine efficiency as an aphrodisiac for men and women with the well known safety record of homoeopathic and herbal medicines. If they are made commercially available by the time this book goes to print, it is intended to mention them in the Sources List.

HYPNOTHERAPY and SELF-HYPNOSIS WITH HOME TAPES

Of all methods available for training and improving the mind, which is a vital component of mastering impotence, hypnosis is by far the best. It is also the most fun. And furthermore, whatever the main reason it is used, in this instance for impotence therapy, it has huge advantages spilling over into other areas as a bonus. It is a technique that offers a whole series of benefits in just one small, easy package.

It is worth getting a few things straight. Hypnosis is not the way it usually appears in movies. It is not necessary for someone to wave hands or shining diamond rings in front of your eyes. At no time are you subjected to the will or command of the hypnotist. At no time is your own will-power lost. At no time can you be made to do something which is against your political, religious, or moral convictions.

Many of the things which make us unhappy can be improved by hypnosis. As unhappiness states are counter-productive in an anti-impotence planning programme, this can only be for personal improvement. Hypnosis can combat numerous kinds of anxieties, phobias and damaging habits. Anxiety over examinations, interviews or a new job, over public speaking or a forthcoming marriage, can all be helped. So can psychological phobias such as those of spiders, enclosed spaces, heights and so on. Emotional problems like underconfidence, blushing, stammering, will also nearly always respond. Hypnosis should also be used in a variety of self-destructive habits like heavy smoking, heavy drinking, and over-eating; these can usually be much improved or stopped altogether by hypnosis.

So can most sexual problems, especially those involved with impotence,.. which is why the subject is dealt with here in such detail. (For even greater help in methods of using self-hypnosis in a variety of ways, see books and manuals on Home Hypnosis in the Sources List).

While most people find it easier to learn hypnosis from an already-trained hypnotherapist, funds are not always available. Even so, money is well spent on learning the techniques of self-hypnosis also known as self-or auto-hypnosis. You can learn it yourself from a tape or from this book very efficiently. However, for those who can afford it, learning from someone else can make the procedure even quicker and easier.

Quite a good idea is to record the following pages of hypnotic induction on your own tape recorder. Played over to yourself at leisure, this will then quickly help you learn to enter the hypnotic state. Some precautions are necessary. It is strongly recommended that the preliminary warning section is recorded at the beginning of the tape. After the warning comes the first and most important part of the learning process, the technique of induction, or achieving hypnosis. Following this should come a period when the therapeutic aims of the session are recorded. In these pages we concentrate on hypnosis as an anti-impotence routine. You could equally easily record other suggestions, scripted by yourself, to achieve other purposes. Several example of this are given in the books just mentioned. Finally, and they are very important indeed, you record the phrases needed in order to bring yourself back to a normal state of consciousness,.. the 'wake-up' signals.

Begin by recording the safety clauses.

"I shall shortly be undergoing induction into hypnosis. This is a safe and brief procedure and will end when I have finished listening to my hypnosis tape. If I wish, I merely have to say that I will wake up in fifteen minutes and I will then awake and be in every way normal. Should I drift off to sleep and not hear the entire recording, then I will sleep peacefully for a few minutes and wake up once again normal in every respect. If the tape recorder should become faulty or should switch off, or if I should become in any way unable to hear it, then I will also wake up at once and be completely normal. At no time will I lose my will-power or my ability to respond swiftly and surely. If there should be any kind of urgent need for my attention, or if there were any form of emergency, I would instantly return to my normal wakeful state, and behave in every way normally and efficiently."

There should now follow a blank period on the tape of about thirty seconds, before induction itself is commenced. Try to record your induction technique in a calm, clear and slow, somewhat monotonous style of speaking. Take plenty of time in the recording, leaving many pauses (rather as when we print the dots sign,.. here). During these the mind can tick over slowly and unhurriedly, absorbing and benefiting from the words heard. You should lie on your bed, preferably in a partly darkened room, or you can sit in a comfortable armchair. Pick a spot on which to focus your eyes. If you are lying flat on your back, look immediately above you on the ceiling,.. then move your eyes up further and select a spot about six inches further back than is the most comfortable spot to look at. If you are going to use this technique regularly, it is a good idea to put a small dot or cross on the ceiling for repeated use.

It is best to use the third person for recordings but the first person is perfectly satisfactory if you prefer it.

Record as follows:-

"Settle back now, thoroughly relaxed. Let your whole body go limp and heavy. Fix your eyes on the spot and relax thoroughly. Soon you are going to relax into a gentle, deep rest. Feel all the tensions of the last few days and the last few hours drain away from you,.. especially from your face and neck and across your shoulder muscles. Feel the tensions drain down your trunk,.. down your arms and legs,.. all the way to your hands and feet,.. your toes and fingers,.. and out ,.. and away. Leaving you relaxed and heavy,.. very still and very peaceful. Just your eyes concentrating still on that same spot.

"As you lie there,.. quiet and relaxed,.. remember that for the next few minutes nothing matters but you relaxing and listening. No other sounds you hear matter at all. No sensations you feel, of your clothing on your body, or textures under your fingers, even of warmth and cold,.. none of these sensations matter at all. If you hear people, or traffic, or any other sounds,.. all these things are just sensations that come and go,.. they don't matter to you,.. so you ignore them completely. You don't let them disturb your rest and relaxing,.. and listening,.. and all the time you are keeping your attention fixed on the spot.

"Lying there,.. quiet and still, you can feel your body living. Your heart beating,.. your lungs breathing,.. your brain thinking,.. your ears listening,.. everything teeming with life,.. yet you are still and peacefully relaxed. Your attention still fixed on the spot. And already you begin to feel your body growing more and more heavy and tired. Every part of you wants to relax,.. and you are going to help it to relax very thoroughly,.. by relaxing in turn every bit of you, starting with your toes and feet.

"Relax the muscles of your toes and feet,.. drain all the strength out of them. Next your calf and shin muscles,.. let them relax too. And then your thighs muscles,.. back and front,.. feel your legs lying very heavy,.. heavy as lead,.. very, very heavy. Let them lie there,.. motionless,.. very heavy,.. very still. Next relax the muscles of your fingers and palms. Then your forearm muscles,.. and your upper arms. So that now your arms, just like your legs, are lying very heavy,.. very heavy,.. as heavy as lead. Next you relax your tummy muscles,.. and your chest muscles. Let your breathing take over automatically, as it will. And all the time your attention is still fixed on that same spot. Gradually your whole body,.. gets more and more heavy, more and more tired. Everything wanting to relax,.. as very soon now it will.

"Now relax the muscles of your buttocks and the small of your back. Feel the strength and the tension drain out of them,.. and the muscles all the way up your spine,.. up between your shoulders,.. and across your shoulders. Everything now, very relaxed,.. very heavy. Your eyelids growing heavy too, wanting to close,.. wanting to close and be peaceful. And soon they will, but just try to concentrate on the spot for a little longer,.. just a little longer, then you can relax and rest. Now relax the muscles up the back of your neck. Feel your head growing heavy. And you relax your face muscles too, and inside your mouth, even your tongue relaxes. Nothing left working but your eyes and those eyes growing heavier and heavier all the time.

"Now I am going to count slowly up to ten. As I do, you will feel yourself relaxing more and more,.. more and more deeply,.. right down, into deep relaxation. Your eyes can close at any time they want to now,.. but anyway, by the time I get to ten, your eyes will be firmly closed and you will be in a gentle state of peaceful, hypnotic rest,.. very relaxed,.. very safe,.. very secure. One,.. two,.. three,.. going deeper and deeper now, deeper and deeper. Four,.. five,.. six,.. very relaxed now,.. very dreamy and drowsy,.. seven,.. eight,.. nine,.. ten. Deeply down now,.. very deeply relaxed,.. very still,.. very safe and very secure. Peacefully relaxed and very still.

"Now I am going to count up to ten once more, and as I do, this time with each count you will feel yourself going even deeper. Deeper and deeper. Very deep,.. right down where it's very deep, very useful,.. very safe. Deeper with every count. One,.. two,.. feeling very sleepy and heavy now,.. three,.. four,.. going deeper and deeper,.. deeper and deeper down,.. five,.. six,.. feeling very dreamy and drowsy now,.. seven,.. eight,.. very sleepy and heavy,.. going down, and down,.. and down,.. going deeper and deeper,.. nine,.. ten. Down you go now, very deep,.. very still,.. very peaceful and relaxed,.. and feeling wonderfully safe and secure."

Some subjects can achieve a considerable level of hypnosis within the first one or two tries of this kind of induction. Others may need six or eight or even a dozen lessons before they start to master it. Sooner or later, however, by trying, preferably once every day, and for ten or fifteen minutes, the technique will be mastered by almost everyone.

It is at this stage that you should insert a section written by yourself and aimed at whatever is your particular problem. For example, you may be trying to overcome bad eating habits which are leading to you being unhappy about your size and weight. Women will find the method very useful for increasing their sexuality and overall interest in and performance in sex generally.

More likely, if you are a man using this programme, you will want to use the hypnosis to help you overcome impotence. Ideally there are two stages for this. The first is aimed to restore and rebuild your confidence deep inside,.. a confidence that is justified but which has been eroded perhaps by the period of impotence. Second stage is a direct attack on the impotence which will gradually remove its stranglehold on the mind of the sufferer.

First the general ego-strengthening section. You might use sentences like the following:-

"Now listen to me,.. listen to my voice. You know that you have started to learn hypnosis for a good reason. You have the motivation and the determination. You are going to embark on an extensive and effective self-help programme,.. a self-improvement programme. Because you want to be better than you are,.. you want to realise your potential,.. a far greater potential than ever before. You have the ability. Deep inside you have plenty of ability, never even used yet. You are going to learn how to use it,.. make it work for you,.. discover its tremendous talents and resources,.. your talents and resources. And now you have made the decision. You are going to be better, stronger, more confident, more capable,.. more happy,.. oh yes, happy, happy, happy,.. happier by far,.. far, far happier. Full of pleasure,.. and contentment,.. and comfort. Full of the happiness that comes from a whole new level of fulfilment.

"All this is going to happen,.. that is absolutely sure. Its going to happen to you,.. not by accident,.. not by magic,.. but because you have decided it. You have decided,.. you will do it,.. you will make it happen. You and your improvement. Your mind,.. your will-power harnessed and working,.. all the time,.. all day,.. every day,.. day-in, day-out. And you will notice it, very soon,.. today even to start with,.. you will feel the changes. Because every day in every way you are going to get better and better,.. every day,.. in every way,.. you,.. getting better and better and better.

"You can feel your mind expanding,.. lifting,.. moving,.. progressing,.. taking control,.. asserting itself. And it will,.. because you have decided it. You have decided it,.. and you are you,.. you are you and you are in charge of you. Only you. And in the whole, huge world there is no-one else quite like you. You are the only one. You are an individual. You are in command. Your strength,.. your control,.. your will-power. And you'll feel it strengthening every day. Little by little control becomes easier,.. easier to exercise command. Your mind moving upward and forward and outward,.. progressing, advancing, learning, improving. Stronger and stronger and stronger.

"And every day too, you'll feel the bad things receding. The things about yourself that bother you,.. they'll all diminish. They won't be so important anymore. They'll be smaller,.. less troublesome,.. they are diminishing because they are becoming more in proportion,.. you are making them come into proportion. No more doubts about yourself and your abilities. No more doubts,.. no hesitations, no fears, no anxieties, no problems and troubles nagging you and overwhelming you. You can face problems,.. improve them,.. solve them. And you won't be bothered by unnatural fears and worries,.. no old anxieties creeping in from the past troubling you, disturbing you, upsetting you. These things are wrong for you. They have no right to bother you,.. so they won't,.. not anymore. Because you won't allow it. Your decision, your strength, and your will-power will not allow it. You are stronger now and getting stronger still. Your will getting stronger,.. strong enough at last. And your will says 'no' to worries and unnatural fears and anxieties. Your will says,.. you will not. You-will-not permit humiliation and doubts and fears and anxieties. So they all recede,.. start fading, coming under control,.. your control.

"And as your will power increase so does your confidence. It grows stronger all the time,.. stronger by the day,.. by the hour. No longer feeling hesitation,.. unsure,.. small,.. uncertain. Oh no,.. that is all gone. Now you are bigger, better, stronger,.. your will-power growing, your mind strengthening, your confidence flowing,.. feeling good,.. feeling strong,.. in control,.. capable. Everything improving, everything developing,.. you improving,.. your mind developing,.. your will power,.. your strength,.. your security,.. your determination,.. your courage. Confidence building, will-power growing, everything advancing,.. progressing. Every day in every way getting better and better,.. you, better and better,.. every day in every way,.. better and better and better still.

"Now listen to me,.. now you know the facts about what can happen to you,.. how you can use your own mind-power,.. your own mind-power,.. to improve yourself and your entire life. Yet there are things holding you back. Secret things. Deep inside things. Things you hardly recognise, perhaps things you try not to think about maybe,.. things of which you tell no-one. These are weighing you down, restricting you, slowing your progress. It is time to be rid of them,.. forever. Everyone has these hidden feelings. You have them,.. they are there, hidden away for years maybe,.. but they are there. And they don't need to be there. They don't deserve to be there. You don't need them. You don't want them. You won't have them,.. how dare they?

"Small doubts,.. small guilts,.. small shames over things that happened long ago. Unfair punishments received,.. insults tolerated,.. physical abuses accepted. Perhaps many many of these tiny, past injustices have lingered and accumulated. And together they weigh too heavily on you. They give you doubts. They make you hesitate. They make you feel unsure,.. uncertain of your abilities,.. uncertain of your reception.

"These are all bad, false, unfair, unneeded,.. they are hangers-on. They are against you. You wish to be rid of them,.. free of them. You want them gone. And that is all it takes. For you to want them gone,.. for you to decide they shall be gone, is enough. That means you examine them. Select each one,.. right now in your mind,.. or later when you are alone. Hold each one up to the light and examine it. Strip it of its hidden mystique,.. its non-existent power. What is it? It is small,.. it is pathetic,.. it is trivial,.. above all it is part of the past. It has no importance any more. So that is it. Out with it. Discover it. Banish it forever. You now see it for what it is,.. nothing. A something that has troubled you for years. But no more. Now you eject it,.. now you reject it. Now you see it in proportion. Now you dispose of it,.. you despise it. You don't fear it,.. you don't even care. You are you. You are in charge, not it. You are done with it. Your mind-power triumphs. It is gone,.. over,.. done with. You care about it no more.

"And at once you feel better. At once the burden lightens. You have won. You can beat every guilt that way,.. one at a time. You can beat every fear that way,.. bit by bit. You can do all these things. Ridding yourself of guilts and shames and anxieties and doubts and fears. They have no part of you now.

"You are a new person,.. stronger character,.. determined fibre,.. filling with courage and determination. Growing better all the time. You are lifting up your head, squaring your shoulders. You are facing facts. You are you. You can look the whole world right in the eye.

"No more hiding. No more doubting. No more retreating or skulking alone inside. But out now, and up, and forward. Greeting the day and the world, greeting everyone with a smile. Knowing there is a place for you right where you choose. You will be better liked, more appreciated. People start to see new things about you, to recognise you for what you are,.. a good, strong, reliable, honest, fair person.

"You know that inside all these things are possible,.. they can all happen,.. more than that, they are already all happening. Already you feel stronger. You feel your confidence growing all the time,.. you ignore set-backs,.. you go right ahead and try again. You keep trying,.. you push on. You never, never give up,.. never yield,.. never doubt.

"You are you,.. you are in charge. Your mind-power knows it, your growing confidence knows it. You are getting bigger, better, stronger, more sure, more fulfilled, more successful, more happy,.. more confident all the time. You are making progress. You are getting better. You,.. you,.. you,.. the very you that deep down inside is you. You are unique,.. you are strong,.. you are positive,.. you are confident. You feel it, you want it, you know it. You,.. you,.. you. Say it over again,.. you,.. you,.. you. You are you. You are you. You are you. Relax and remember that. Relax and remember that. Relax and remember. Relax,.. relax deeply now,.. very deeply,.. relax,.. very deeply,.. and remember. Relax and remember.

"Remember too that everything good that happens to you, happens not as result of someone else,.. or something else. Not even this lesson does that. It all happens because of you. Because your new found strength, your new confidence works for you. You are making it happen.

"Everything happens because you decided it,.. you willed it. In yourself, feeling good and content and happy. Feeling fit and strong and healthy and well. Feeling your body teeming with life and zest and energy,.. ready to move,.. ready to go,.. tuning up,.. feeling good,.. really good. Feeling happy, feeling joy and satisfaction,.. feeling exhilaration,.. feeling light and buoyant,.. full of pleasure and happiness. Your mind happy and contented,.. your body strong and vigorous,.. feeling altogether fit and strong and healthy and well,.. and oh, so wonderfully good and happy.

"And every day when you practise you'll go to your quiet place and relax. You'll look at your chosen spot and let your mind and body go calm and still. You'll relax your entire body, bit by bit, as you just did, until everything feels limp and heavy. Then, slowly but surely you'll count yourself down into relaxation,.. deep, gentle, hypnotic rest and relaxation.

"Then, when you are in that comfortable and safe and secure state, you will remind yourself of these things,.. several times over.

"You can do it,.. you are doing it,.. your mind-power is in control because you are you,.. you are you, and you alone are in charge of you. The bad things are diminishing and leaving you,.. no more worries now,.. now fears, no doubts, no anxieties,.. no fretting and worrying.

"And you yourself are getting better,.. progressing in every way and every day. Your personality advancing, your confidence growing, your will-power expanding,.. everything improving and getting better and better,.. feeling fit and strong and healthy and well,.. and safe,.. and certain,.. and confident,.. and contented,.. and happier,.. happier all the time,.. you're feeling happy,.. happy,.. happy,.. happy."

(Pause for several seconds).

The sexual formula

At this point the second stage, the part dealing directly with the impotence (or some other problem) is inserted to continue the practice session. Say,..

"Now listen to me. Now you know the facts about what can happen to you,... how you can use your mind-power,.. your own mind power to improve yourself and your entire life.

"This is especially right in dealing with your problem. Because your problem was not caused by you. It was caused by others. It isn't right. It isn't fair. It is not part of you,.. the real natural you. It doesn't belong. This problem,.. this sexual limitation doesn't belong in you. It came from the past, it came from others. It has lived in you, making you feel bad,.. making you ashamed, unhappy,.. uncertain for far too long. And now that is all going to change. Now you are entering a new phase. Now you see it for what it is,.. wrong,.. unfair,.. outdated,.. and you are just not going to put up with it any longer.

"When you were born, you were born normal,.. you were born healthy and normal, and left to yourself you would have grown and gone on growing that way. You would have grown into a normal, healthy sexual man. That was what was right. That was what nature intended. You would have learned about sex, been motivated properly by sex, been able to have sex, look forward to sex and enjoy it, and perform normally and naturally. But that was denied you. It was denied you not because you deserved it,.. not because you did something wrong,.. not because you were at fault. Not at all. Not because there was anything wrong with you. No, it was denied you by others,.. other people spread their own sick, distorted mistakes into you when you were small,.. when you were too young to understand or to resist.

"As you grew up you developed all the correct, natural instincts of your body and your mind. You developed sexual interests too,.. those all-powerful, vital, naturally implanted instincts,.. everything would have been alright,.. but the way you lived,.. the rules that were imposed on you stopped all that. Normal ideas were suppressed. Normal thoughts and habits were discouraged. Everything to do with sex, you were taught to be wrong and dirty and nasty and wicked and evil.

"You were taught wrongly. But you were a child. You knew no better. You did as you were told. You believed as you were told. You became what you were told. All the suppressions, impositions, punishments,.. the forbiddings, the rules, the denials,.. all were pressed into your young mind until they had you fully in their grasp. These things held you, against your natural instincts,.. against your wishes. And they held you tight,.. and right up until now they have had their effect.

"Yet these things are false. They are distorted,.. twisted,.. sick,.. and wrong. They distorted your knowledge,.. your mind,.. your behaviour. They stored up trouble in your young mind. It was a wicked thing but people did it in those days,.. they still do. They still teach that sex is bad and dirty whereas really it is thrilling and beautiful and natural.

"Now, all that confused thinking,.. all that wrongly imposed reaction poisoned your young mind. You couldn't help it,.. you didn't know. Instead of growing strong and confident and relaxed with your sexuality, you developed doubts,.. anxieties and fears, guilts. You had natural sexual feelings but you thought they were wrong. You wanted to do sexual things but you thought they were indecent. You were confused. Full of conflicts. And the doubts meant failure. To you sex was not respectable,.. it was furtive, secretive and wrong. All those false fears,.. false thoughts,.. false teachings brought you to failure.

"You got sexually interested,.. and excited,.. you wanted to go ahead. Your body responded,.. your hormones developed you,.. your sex organs responded,.. you got desires and erections and the impulse to go ahead and use them. Your body was doing well. But deep in your mind the doubts and confusions raged,.. the protective barriers went up,.. the falsehoods triumphed. They prevented your body from completing its response,.. remember that,.. years and years later,.. the falsehoods of others planted in your mind blocked the natural responses of your body. Without those falsehoods you would have been fine. Remember this now,.. remember this in every detail,.. it was and is the falsehoods of others planted in your mind that block your body from its natural successful responses. That is it in a nutshell.

"And now that stage is all over. The road back to healthy, normal, natural sex performance starts today,.. right here and right now. And it starts because of you.

"Now you see those past failures for what they are,.. the results of twisted, distorted thinking. The result of the tricking of a young child's mind. The result of unnatural guilts and anxieties.

"Now you have demolished the false thinking. Now you know better. Now you see right through the stupidity of the false logic,.. the ridiculous prohibitions of society. Now you know sex is normal and healthy and natural. It does not harm you. It does not harm your partner. She is naturally built and equipped for sex too. It is correct and decent and clean and wholesome for you to have and enjoy sex. To be able to carry out the full sexual act like the man you are.

"And you are no longer that child,.. that child that accepted the nonsense poured into it. Now you are grown. Now you are a man. Now you think and decide and act for yourself. Now you refuse to be conditioned by the old rubbish. Now you see the right path. Now you can go ahead.

"So, the confused mess of the past is over. Now you have no misunderstandings. Now your fear and guilts and doubts are receding. Now your anxieties are calming down,.. fading away,.. disappearing,.. leaving you. You are chasing them off, replacing them with healthy, normal thoughts and sexual appetites. Now you know you are a responsible man doing his own thinking.

"You are no longer going to be made a victim of the past,.. of lies and nonsense,.. of your own youthful helplessness. Now you are strong. Now you are confident. Now you are free,.. unfettered,.. unconfused. Now you know you should feel sexual,.. now you know you need and want sex because it is good. Now you know your erections and sex interests are there and they are good and strong and healthy and natural. Now you start to feel good, to feel better,.. to feel that growing strength and confidence in yourself,.. in your sexual abilities,.. in your sexual performance,.. in the size and strength and staying power of your erections. You know it is good,.. it feels good,.. That erection is good for you,.. and good for your partner. It is good and right and very, very natural for you to have an erection, to use it and to enjoy it. It is natural to feel it enter your partner,.. for her to see it, touch it, play with it, caress it,.. welcome it into her body as nature intended.

"Now everyone who knows about sexual matters has explained to you,.. they tell you sex is right and good,.. they tell you you are normal to feel sexual, normal to have big strong, sustained erections,.. normal to use those erections. All this because it is right and normal and decent and natural. It is permitted,.. no longer denied and forbidden,.. it is permitted. You have full permission for good, healthy sex.

"Every day you will practice with your erection,.. either alone or with your partner. You will find it will get easier and better all the time. Each time stronger, each time more sustained, each time feeling more natural. It will get better and better in every way.

"And each day when you have your hypnosis practice, once you are relaxed, you will remind yourself of these things.

"Your problem is not your fault,.. it was caused by others. Your problem is not normal and natural for you. You are you and you are now in charge of you,.. and you and everyone else gives you full and total permission for sex. Remember that from now on your erection will be growing stronger,.. bigger,.. will feel better,.. will penetrate easier,.. painlessly and smoothly,.. bringing pleasures not harm to you and your partner. Your erection will last and last,.. it will enter your partner safely and comfortably,.. you can move it in her as much as you like,.. as long as you like. Its strength and length will be retained, better and better each day,.. and it will be sustained longer and longer,.. long enough for you to climax,.. to ejaculate deep inside your partner in the normal, healthy, way.

"And as all this starts to happen your confidence will grow even more along with it,.. every day stronger,.. every day greater will-power,.. greater strength, and determination,.. everything about you,.. your brain, your confidence, your personality,.. your manhood, all expanding and improving,.. all the time. And you will feel calm, and good and confidant,.. and very, very happy.

"And later, when you count yourself awake again it will be with the lasting knowledge that you are winning, at last. You have been strong enough. You feel proud,.. and strong,.. and confident,.. and happy about yourself and your growing potency. Relax now and remember that. Relax and remember that. Relax and remember,.. relax,.. very deeply down now,.. very deeply,.. relax,.. deeply down and relaxing,.. and remember. Relax and remember."

When you have completed the training session, it is important not to attempt simply to get up and walk away. This can leave you in a light hypnotic trance in which your actions may be inefficient and forgetful. It is vital therefore, to go through the simple process of returning to normal using the 'wake-up' signal method. You should use a rather more brisk voice as you record the following in the usual way.

"I am now going to count from ten back down to one. As I do you will feel yourself getting lighter and lighter, returning towards the surface,.. until at number one you will have your eyes wide open, and you will feel fresh and wide awake and alert. And you'll feel very glad that you did it. Next time you will find it easier still,.. ten,.. nine,.. eight,.. seven,.. starting to come up now,.. up towards the surface,.. six,.. five,.. four, coming right up to the top now,.. starting to wake up,.. three,.. two,.. one,.. eyes open,.. wide awake,.. fresh and alert."

Once the session is thoroughly completed by this return procedure, you should remain sitting or lying for just a few seconds until you are completely back to normal.

SEX PROBLEM BOOKLETS

A series of short booklets has been produced concerning specific sexual problems. They were compiled by a group of doctors and members of associated professions and they represent the latest techniques for personal treat-yourself-at-home methods for combating sexual problems. One is a very brief and correspondingly inexpensive summary of this book and which thoroughly and conciseley covers the treatment of impotence. There is also a very good one concerned with increasing the low female libido. There is one about treating premature ejaculation and another that explains vaginismus and how to overcome it. They are excellent publications and many people have found they are all that were needed. (See Sources List).

PENIS EXERCISES

Part of the Penatone Programme mentioned above involves training the muscles of the penis and its surrounding supportive tissues. For those wise enough to embark on Penatone routines the next section is superfluous. However, for those lacking the funds to invest in Penatone, the following exercises will be found most advantageous. Many men have found them practically miraculous in generating more sexual control and the intensification of ejaculations.

1. In this exercise you will be building specific penis muscles. These are the muscles that 'clench' your urine off when you have finished emptying the bladder. It involves the tough muscles you can feel behind the scrotum. Contracting this muscle when the penis is erect causes it to jerk. Strong muscles mean more thrill to your partner. Also, as these muscles are partly responsible for ejaculation, training them means

more pleasure for you too. Contract the muscles by squeezing (clenching) several times in quick succession. Because the action is quite invisible, you may practise it several times a day whenever you are driving, at the office, and so on. After a series of about six rapid contractions and relaxations, give one final contraction and sustain it while you count to ten seconds.

2. This flexibilty and mobility exercise requires an erect penis. Even if you cannot achieve an erection, move the penis down between the legs as far as it will comfortably go. Then put it up against the abdomen. Next, move it to the left as far as is comfortable, then to the right. Now move it in its maximum full circle. Repeat this three times per exercise period the first week, ten times the second week and twenty times in subsequent weeks.
3. Again with the penis erect, stand with the feet astride. Loosely encircle the penis with a short, wide rubber band. Hold the penis up so that the rubber band, gripped by finger and thumb, is touching your abdomen. You are, as it were, pulling the penis towards the body with the band. Perform the clenching action. The penis will be seen to pull away against the tension of the rubber. Repeat a dozen times.

These exercises strengthen the muscles involved in sexual activity. These muscles are the same ones that are used to control the flow of urine from the bladder, but, at the same time, the more you exercise, the stronger the muscles will get, and your sex life will be greatly enhanced. By contracting the penis in this manner, you can further stimulate the woman during intercourse by flicking and tickling her high in the vagina. Practising these sex muscles exercises can thus provide added sexual benefits for both man and woman.

And there is an additional exciting benefit for men who conscientiously practise these exercises. It's called multiple orgasm. Up until recently it was believed that all men have a period of recovery, called a refractory period, during which time they cannot be sexually aroused or perform sex, following an initial sex act. This period usually lasts anywhere from a few minutes to an hour or more. Women do not have this refractory period, and many are capable of having multiple orgasms, one after the other, especially if they train to that purpose. The exciting news is the discovery by two Californian researchers, that some men too are capable of having multiple orgasms, defined as repeated orgasms without ejaculation, except for the final orgasm which is simultaneous with ejaculation. According to Dr. Gordon D. Jensen, (Professor of Psychiatry and Paediatrics, School of Medicine, University of California at Davis), and his associate Dr. Mina Robbins, (Associate Professor of Human Development, California State University, Sacramento), some men can have repeated orgasms independently of ejaculation. They are able to exercise control over their ejaculation, and thus experience anywhere from three to ten orgasms prior to their final orgasm with ejaculation. This discovery is most significant because it runs counter to the belief, which had been considered scientific gospel, that orgasm and ejaculation can only be one continuous process in the male. It also created the possibility that more men, by experimenting and learning to control their ejaculatory response, will be able to achieve the ultimate goal,... multiple orgasms without refractory periods. Perhaps by becoming expert in the Sex Muscle Exercises, the men involved were able to exercise expert control over their ejaculatory response, and succeed in delaying it until they had achieved multiple orgasms prior to ejaculation.

Once you have become proficient in the sexual exercises outlined here, you will be able to 'clench' or control these muscles just as orgasm occurs. By doing this, the amount of semen discharged at ejaculation is decreased. You can thus retain some of the ejaculate by using the squeeze technique. When you feel you are about to ejaculate, remove your penis from the vagina and squeeze the tip until the desire to ejaculate ceases. Then reinsert. Clearly this practise requires an informed and co-operative partner as otherwise the repeated withdrawals may impair her enjoyment of the proceedings.

In time, and with practice and perseverance, more and more men will be able to do likewise and achieve super potency, perhaps multiple orgasmic capacity, and once again recruit limp, even 'retired' muscles and other tissues, back into full action.

CONCLUSION

The pages of this book have tried to offer a thorough guide to the bitter problem of sexual impotence. We have discovered the causes and the origins of those causes. We have demonstrated the astonishing prevalence of impotence throughout the world.

We have shown too that impotence has many possible routes to successful treatment. We have held out great and justified hope, even to the worst cases, that there is a way to success. A few weeks of preparatory training concluding with the Twenty Minute Method has worked for huge numbers of sufferers. It can work for you.

So now you know the how and the why of the problem and the why and the how of the solution.

The suggestion we make to patients is the same here as we do in the Consulting Room. Read the book, discuss it and make the decision to start. This will give you time to organise further reading or to obtain any items you feel you will need. Plan the re-training well in advance, deciding on a specific, target day on which to start,.. then give it the same degree of top priority you would give to any other medical therapy of high-level importance. Then go for it, patiently but thoroughly and determinedly. That way not only can it work for you, it WILL work for you.

* * *

Bibliography:

Becoming Orgasmic; by Heinman and Lopiccolo.
Pub. Prentice-Hall,1976

Will You Still Love Me? Pub. Age Concern,(Media Unit)
1268 London Rd., London, SW16 4EJ

* * *

Books/manuals from present author and/or colleagues:

Books:

The Twenty Minute Miracle for Men.
(Home Therapy for Impotence)

The Penis.
(Explains Penis Training and Enlarging)

AGE and SEX.
(A Manual for Sex-Life in the Over-Forties)

Play-Safe Sex.
(How a varied sex-life can be achieved despite today's dangers)

SEXUAL FILE-of-FACTS.
(Self-selected manual from seventy favourite subjects)

The Love Book of Erotic Short Stories

I Can Make You Happy... in Three Days.
(Home Hypnotherapy and Self-Hypnosis)

Booklets and Manuals:

Sexual Problem Series:
Erectile Inadequacy. (Impotence)
Increasing Female Libido. (Frigidity)
Premature Ejaculation.

Aphrodisiacs for All

Adaptogenics, the New Road to Health

All available from:
BabyShoe Publications (Medical),
1,The Butchery, Sandwich,
Kent, C13 9DL, England.

Sources:

For the convenience of readers full details and supplies concerning the following listed products and services from the text of this book can now all be arranged through the central address below:-

ACTIVE, Swedish Erection Device
Energising Rings
GYNATONE, Pelvic Floor Programme
Hypnotherapy, Personal Cassettes
MASCULONE and FEMINONE, Sexual Anti-Sera Suppositories
PENATONE Penis Training (and Enlarging) Programme
READY, Swedish Erection Maintaining Rings
Regenerative Therapy

from:
Dipix Distributions,
PO Box 75, Sandwich,
Kent, CT13 9RT, England.

* * *

Latex and Leather Clothing
Designs in Leather, 3, Leigham Court Dr.,
Leigh on Sea, Essex, SS9 1PS, U.K.

Sexual Aids
Erotic Tapes, Films, Magazines
Valentine Products, PO Box 63
Feltham, Middx., TW13 7QN, U.K.
or
Magic Moments, 14, Rock Close,
Hastings, E.Sussex, TN35 4JW, U.K.

Erotic Lingerie and PlayWear
East of Eden, 1, Clerkenwell Rd.,
London EC1.
or
Lovecare, 326, Oxford Rd.,
Reading, Berks., RG3 1AF, U.K.

Female Protective Condoms, (Femidom)
Chartex International, U.K.

Useful Addresses:

Amarant Trust:
30 Lambeth Road, London, SE1 7PN. Tel:081-200-0200.
Promotes better understanding of the menopause and hormone replacement therapy.

Arthritis Care:
5, Grosvenor Crescent, London, SW1X 7ER. Tel:071-235-0902.
Offers information and support on all aspects of coping with arthritis. 468 local branches.

Association to Aid the Sexual and Personal Relationships of People with a Disability (SPOD):
286 Camden Road, London, N7 OBJ. Tel:071-607-8851/2.
SPOD provides an advisory and counselling service for people with disabilities who are in sexual difficulty.

Divorce Conciliation and Advisory Service:
38 Ebury Street, London, SW1 0LU. Tel:071 730 2422.
Offers counselling and conciliation services at any stage of divorce proceedings. Free for all those on social security.

Relate (National Marriage Guidance):
Herbert Gray College, Little Church Street, Rugby, Warwickshire, CV21 3AP. Tel:0788-73241.
Sees numerous couples over 60 who find discussing their problems with a counsellor enormously helpful.

* * *